the EDIBLE HEIRLOOM GARDEN

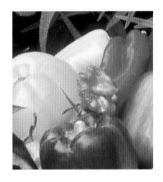

Rosalind Creasy

PERIPLUS

D1295751

First published in 1999 by
Periplus Editions (HK) Ltd.,
with editorial offices at 153 Milk Street,
Boston, Massachusetts 02109 and
5 Little Road #08-01
Singapore 536983.

Library of Congress Cataloging-in-Publication Data
 Creasy, Rosalind.
     The edible heirloom garden / by Rosalind Creasy--1st ed.
            p.   cm.
     Includes bibliographical references (p.   )
     ISBN 962-593-941(paper)
     1. Vegetables -- Heirloom varieties. 2. Vegetable gardening.
 3. Cookery.(Vegetables)   I. Title.
     SB324.73.C74 1999
     635--DC21   98-41027
                                          CIP

Distributed by

USA
Charles E. Tuttle Co., Inc.
RR 1 Box 231-5
North Clarendon, VT 05759
Tel: (802) 773-8930
Tel: (800) 526-2778

CANADA
Raincoast Books
8680 Cambie Street
Vancouver, Canada V6P 6M9
Tel: (604) 323-7100
Fax: (604) 323-2600

SOUTHEAST ASIA
Berkeley Books Pte. Ltd.
5 Little Road #08-01
Singapore 536983
Tel: (65) 280-3320
Fax: (65) 280-6290

JAPAN
Tuttle Shokai Ltd.
1-21-13, Seki
Tama-ku, Kawasaki-shi
Kanagawa-ken 214, Japan
Tel: (044) 833-0225
Fax: (044) 822-0413

First edition
05 04 03 02 01 00 99
10 9 8 7 6 5 4 3 2 1

Design by Kathryn Sky-Peck

PRINTED IN SINGAPORE

contents

heirloom vegetable gardens

Seeds are a link to the past. Immigrants smuggled them into this country in the lining of their suitcases, under the bands of their hats, and in the hems of their dresses. The Germans brought cabbages, the Italians paste tomatoes, and the Mexicans their beloved chiles. According to Kent Whealy, director of the Seed Savers Exchange (an organization dedicated to saving old vegetable varieties), from the time of the *Mayflower* to that of the boat people, many of our heirloom seeds have entered the country in just this way.

The home gardens in which these seeds were grown a hundred years ago

A few years ago, I grew an heirloom vegetable garden filled with varieties that would have been grown in America in the late 1800s. My scarecrow, Millie, (*left*) oversaw the garden. The wheelbarrow contains much produce from that garden. The seed catalog (*above*) is from the late 1800s as are the bean varieties.

differed greatly from home gardens today. For one thing, the varieties themselves were notably diverse—for example, there were high-shouldered tomatoes (whose tops protrude above the stems), purple broccoli, and huge, dense beets. Even within varieties, the produce was much less uniform than what we're used to. But an even more fundamental difference relates to the seeds themselves: when planting time

came, gardeners took seeds not from commercial packages but from jars in closets where the seeds had been stored from the previous year's harvest. Gardeners in the olden days used the seeds of their own open-pollinated plants—varieties capable of reproducing themselves.

By the 1930s, commercially marketed seeds of many new varieties were becoming increasingly available to home gardeners. Many new hybrids proved to be more vigorous, uniform, and widely adaptable than some of the open-pollinated varieties, and the public accepted them enthusiastically. However, people could not save the hybrid seeds to plant the next year. To produce a hybrid variety, a breeder crosses two varieties or even two species of plants. But like the mule—a cross between a donkey and a horse—hybrids cannot reproduce themselves, so the seed companies must repeat the crossing process every year.

1

Commercially produced varieties streamlined the home garden, simplifying planting and standardizing produce, but in the process, old, open-pollinated varieties cultivated for generations disappeared. Some horticulturalists estimate that thousands of plant varieties have been lost forever.

For the better part of the past fifty years, American gardeners have favored many of these commercial varieties and hybrids, but change is in the air. Gardeners are by no means forsaking them, and no one is denying that the heavy production and uniformity of some hybrids make them appealing, but many old, open-pollinated varieties are drawing attention. Diversity in all its glory is coming to be valued anew. Against the backdrop of ever spreading monocultures—huge

single-variety crops—the old varieties show their unusual shapes, colors, and sizes to great advantage. Gardeners and cooks have rediscovered small yellow plum tomatoes, blue cornmeal, and rich yellow fingerling potatoes. Restaurants use orange tomatoes in their salads and 'Dragon Langerie' beans—yellow romano beans with maroon lace markings—for a splash of the unusual on their appetizer plates.

Collectively, these plants are known as heirloom varieties—varieties "of special value handed on from one generation to another," as *Webster's* defines the word *heirloom*. More specifically, most seed people agree that the term applies to any open-pollinated variety that is more than fifty years old.

Some gardeners are primarily interested in the taste of the heirloom vari-

eties, the 'Bonny Best' tomato, for example. Other gardeners enjoy the novelty of heirlooms and like to amuse the family by serving 'Mortgage Lifter' tomatoes, 'Ruth Bible' beans, and 'Howling Mob' corn or to arrive at a Fourth of July picnic with red, white, and blue potato salad made with regu-

---

Vegetables are not the only endangered cultured plants, the old flower varieties are in trouble too. I planted many of them in my heirloom vegetable garden including (*bottom*) the species white zinnias, calliopsis, and gloriosa daisies.
Another view of my heirloom garden (*right*) shows more of the old flowers and the chicken coop. It includes the single, tall, cream Peruvian and single species white zinnias; tansy, with its fernlike foliage in the foreground; strawberry gomphrena; tall status; species yellow marigolds; and a magenta plume celosia from Monticello.

lar potatoes and blue and red heirloom potatoes. Still others appreciate the historical connections—the 'Mayflower' beans or 'Mandan Bride' corn, for instance, or a lettuce variety brought to this country by a great-great-grandmother.

I have been gardening and cooking with unusual varieties for as long as I can remember. Over the years, that especially tasty corn variety, that unusual-colored bean, and those vegetables with offbeat names pleased my soul, and I sought them out. But my interest was really piqued almost twenty years ago at a conference on seed saving. I met other heirloom-variety gardeners who gave me a different slant on the subject. Many had been drawn to these vegetables and fruits initially by their novelty and taste but soon became concerned—as I did— about a more global issue: the erosion

of the vast gene pool of vegetables.

To stay in existence, plant varieties must be grown and kept growing. Our bank of irreplaceable vegetables from which future breeds will draw has shrunk alarmingly.

It's critical that we now focus on this erosion and start to rebuild the endangered stock. The U.S. government and the seed companies are cooperating to save some varieties in storage facilities, but the bulk of the vegetable-seed-saving effort rests with the home gardener. Fortunately, reversing the trend does not require sacrifice. Instead, as this book attests, it can be a fascinating adventure both in the garden and at the table.

No matter what draws you to the preservation effort, it's only fair to mention a few caveats. Many heirloom vegetables have been selected and

maintained to match old-fashioned cooking and storage methods. From a modern standpoint, this often means using "stringy" string beans that have a great "beany" flavor or huge "keeper" carrots that, while they are a bit unwieldy to store and cook, are incomparable roasted in the embers of a fire or baked. Of course, part of the great fascination is preparing dishes that are rich in taste and color as well as represent a slice of living history.

Heirlooms are the focus of this book and make an exciting, even absorbing, theme garden by themselves. But my research and my own gardening experience have shown me that the venerable old varieties have a place in any garden. Growing an heirloom garden is a way to focus on these treasures, but the true place of heirloom vegetables is wherever gardens grow.

3

how to grow an heirloom garden

Heirloom varieties are not necessarily rare. You probably already grow a number of them—for example, 'Kentucky Wonder' beans, 'Black Beauty' eggplant, 'Pearson' tomatoes, and 'Yellow Crookneck' squash are all heirlooms. You could fill a garden completely with common heirlooms, but my purpose here is to explore the uncommon and even unique possibilities of an heirloom garden. By growing an heirloom garden you can have the fun of growing unusual and tasty vegetables, keep alive the less common varieties, and learn how to save some of your own seeds.

Choosing and Obtaining Heirlooms

Let's look at how to choose and obtain some of the rarer varieties. Read through An Encyclopedia of Heirloom Vegetables (page 21) for descriptions of various varieties and then choose a handful that appeal to you. To keep things simple, choose only six to eight varieties to start with. Since you are probably planning to save your seeds, you might want to begin with the vegetables whose seeds are easiest to save: beans, tomatoes, peppers, and lettuces. Assuming you haven't yet grown any of these varieties, I recommend that you treat your heirloom garden as an experiment. After all, you won't know when you start out how well these varieties are going to perform in your particular climate.

With a few exceptions, plan, plant, and maintain an heirloom garden the same way you would any other modern vegetable garden. For information on how to install a vegetable garden from scratch, details on maintenance, and solutions to pests and diseases problems, see Appendices A and B (pages 90–101). You should know that, compared with modern varieties, some heirloom vegetables are more disease-prone (for instance, some of the cucumbers and peas), less productive

Heirloom vegetables (*right*), primarily from my heirloom garden include: 'Blackstone' watermelons with their thick rind for pickling; 'Brandywine' tomatoes; 'Dr. Martin's' and 'King of the Garden' limas; 'Rouge Vif d'Etampes,' 'Flat White,' and 'Sugar' pumpkins; 'Long Island Improved' Brussels Sprouts; and numerous gourds.

(some of the colored potatoes in particular), and less uniform in their ripening times, shapes, and colors.

You may have to order some of the more unusual heirlooms by mail. Most local nurseries carry only a limited selection, so for the rarer old vegetables, such as 'Cherokee' beans or 'Dad's Mug' tomatoes, you'll have to obtain seed from companies that specialize in heirlooms (see Resources page 102). To explore heirloom varieties further—perhaps to locate a specific variety you remember as a child or to track down one of the really rare ones—contact the seed exchanges.

Seed exchanges, either membership organizations such as the Seed Savers Exchange, or informal ones run by seed companies like Seeds Blüm, are grassroots networks of dedicated gardeners who trade seeds of unusual and threatened open-pollinated vegetable varieties. To use an exchange you become a member or obtain a catalog and select varieties of seeds offered by an individual gardener. You then mail a self-addressed stamped envelope to the people offering the seeds. If they still have seeds they will send some to you. In many exchanges seeds are traded, and you will need to offer varieties from your garden in order to be listed; in others there is no such limitation.

Keep in mind that seed exchanges are primarily trading organizations for preserving the seed bank, not commercial seed companies, so inventory varies from year to year and among exchanges. A hint: for the largest selection of varieties, trade seeds in these organizations early in the year before most of the choice varieties are gone.

Saving Seeds

I never even thought about saving my own seeds when I started vegetable gardening thirty years ago. As far as I was concerned, seeds came in beautiful packages, not from my plants. I find myself amazed at how simple and satisfying the process is. For example, I merely keep a few 'Dutch White' runner beans each year for next year's crop. I make sure they are completely dry, freeze them for a day to kill any weevil eggs, package them, label them, and put them away. That's all there is to it. I felt like a chump for having ordered new seeds of open-pollinated

varieties every spring when I could have easily saved my own.

Though the seed-saving process is easy, some background is essential. To select and save seeds, you have to know some elementary botany, and you have to practice some trial and error. That's why I suggest that you start simply, with only a few heirloom varieties.

Let's begin with a review of the birds-and-bees information that people think they already know (until they're

My heirloom garden (*above*) contained many different varieties of lima beans including; 'Dr. Martin's,' 'King of the Garden,' 'Christmas,' and 'Fordhook Giant.' 'Brandywine' tomatoes (*left*) I purchased while in the Brandywine Valley in Pennsylvania were the best I'd ever eaten. David Cavagnaro (*right*), once manager of the Seed Saver's garden in Decorah, Iowa, harvests beans for me to sample.

called upon to explain it). The reproduction of seed plants involves pollination—the transference of pollen, which contains the sperm cells (produced by the stamen), to the stigma, which contains the ovary. Once a plant has been pollinated, seeds form. If the pollen from a flower fertilizes the ovary of the same flower, the process is called self-pollination. To self-pollinate, a flower must have both stamen and stigma; such a flower is called a perfect flower. Beans and peas have perfect flowers and usually self-pollinate. When pollen is transferred, either between flowers on the same plant or between plants, the process is called cross-pollination. Pollen is carried from flower to flower either by an insect or by the wind. Corn, squash, melons, and beets are all cross-pollinated.

The aim of seed saving is to preserve existing varieties unaltered, to prevent the plant from cross-pollinating with a different variety. Suppose you have a 'Jack-O'-Lantern' pumpkin plant situated next to a zucchini plant. A bee might visit a male flower of the pumpkin plant and then fly over to a female flower of the zucchini plant, thus transferring pollen from one plant to the other—that is, cross-pollinating the zucchini and the pumpkin. (The resulting cross-pollinated zucchini and pumpkin fruits will not be affected until the next generation.) When you plant the seed from the cross-pollinated squash the next year, the result will be a cross between the two. Sometimes that cross produces a good offspring (that's one way to get new varieties), but usually you'll just

get a weird squash. I remember letting some squash plants that had sprouted in the compost pile mature. I got a cross between a striped summer ball squash and an acorn squash: a striped, tough-skinned, stringy summer squash.

When you intend to save seeds in order to perpetuate a variety, you must always take steps to prevent cross-pollination when you plan your garden.

With plants that have perfect flowers and usually pollinate themselves before they open (such as beans), cross-pollination is seldom a problem. Others, such as those in the squash family, cross-pollinate readily, so they must be isolated to ensure that the variety remains pure.

There are a number of ways to isolate plants. First, if your garden is not near your neighbors', plant only one

variety of each type of vegetable, since pollination does not occur among different genera. Or plant potential cross-pollinators far apart from each other (some varieties need be separated by only a hundred feet, while others require half a mile). For instance, if you and your neighbors grow different varieties of squash or corn within three hundred feet of each other, you won't be able to save seeds, since the pollen from the other varieties will be carried to your plants. A physical barrier might work to isolate your heirlooms: rows of tall corn between species of peppers, for example, or a building standing between your potential cross-pollinators.

Another fundamental point is one I touched on earlier: saving the seeds of hybrids is wasted energy, since hybrid plants don't reproduce themselves. You have to know which plants are open-pollinated varieties that give viable offspring and which are hybrids. (To prevent confusion, seed companies label hybrids and F1 hybrids, a form of hybrid, on their seed packets and in their catalogs.)

Finally, you have to know the life cycle of your plants. While most of our vegetables are annuals (maturing in one season), many are biennials, meaning they take two seasons to reproduce. Some popular biennials are beets, carrots, and parsley. With biennials, you get no seeds the first growing season.

With these basic botanical concepts under your belt, there are a few more particulars to master for seed saving:

Saving seeds as shown here at Old Sturbridge Village (*top*) was a necessity in Colonial times as there were few seed companies. In the Seed Saver's garden (*bottom*) in Decorah, Iowa the peppers and eggplants are 'caged' to prevent bees from cross pollinating the plants and contaminating the varieties. The seed room at the Seed Savers (*right, bottom*) contains the seeds of hundreds of bean varieties all cataloged and sealed in jars.

1. Learn to recognize plant diseases, since some (particularly viruses) are transmitted in seeds.

2. Always label your seed rows and seed containers; your memory can play tricks on you.

3. Never plant all your seeds at once, lest the elements wipe them out.

4. Learn to select the best seeds for the next generation. Select seeds from the healthiest plants and from those producing the best vegetables.

5. To maintain a strong gene pool, select seeds from a number of plants, not just one or two. (This does not apply to self-pollinating varieties; see "Saving Bean Seeds" below.)

6. Get to know the vegetable families, since members of the same family often cross-pollinate. (A list of vegetable families is included in Appendix A, with the information on crop rotation. See page 90.)

7. Only mature, ripe seeds will be viable. Learn what such seeds look like for all your vegetables.

Everyone interested in seed saving will benefit from reading *Seed to Seed*, by Suzanne Ashworth. She gives detailed instructions on how to save seeds of all kinds of vegetables.

Saving Bean Seeds

Beans are the easiest vegetable seeds to save. Since they are mostly self-pollinating, you'll be able to grow two or three varieties with few cross-pollination problems. Still, plant varieties that are very different next to each

other. Then, if any crossing does occur, the resulting seed will usually look different from the original, and you'll know that the variety has been altered.

Plant and care for your bean plants as you would ordinarily. When harvest time approaches, choose eight or ten of the plants that are among the healthiest. With snap beans, leave a dozen or so pods on each plant to mature and cook the rest. Let dry-bean types mature as usual. Beans usually ripen from bottom to top. Pick the pods as they start to crack, or the seeds will fall out onto the ground, where they will probably get wet and start to rot.

Do not save seeds from diseased plants. Diseases borne by bean seeds are anthracnose and bacterial blight. Symptoms of anthracnose are small brown spots that enlarge to become sunken black spots. Bacterial blight is characterized by dark green spots on the pods, which slowly become dry and brick red.

The most bothersome pest of bean seeds is the weevil. After you dry your bean seeds thoroughly (see below), pack them in a mason jar (or a like container), label them, and freeze them for twenty-four hours to kill any weevils. Then put them in a cool dark place. (See "An Encyclopedia of Heirloom Vegetables," page 21, for information on saving the seeds of lettuces, peppers, and tomatoes.)

Storing Seeds

Beans are the easiest seeds to save—others require a little more effort. Seeds must be stored carefully to ensure germination the next season. The greatest enemy of seed viability is moisture, so you must dry the seeds thoroughly before storing them. Lay them out on a screen in a warm, dry room for a few weeks, stirring them every few days. Biting a seed is a good test: if you can't dent it, it's probably dry enough.

Another problem is heat. Seeds must be stored in a cool, dry, dark place, but many can be frozen if they're dried properly and placed in a sealed container. They will stay viable for years in a freezer if they're properly packaged in an airtight freezer bag. (Don't freeze bean or pea seeds, though. They need more air than freezing permits.)

heirloom garden style

The farms at Old Sturbridge Village (*right*) are recreations of Colonial farmsteads. The gardens are filled with heirloom vegetables and fruits and visitors are treated to both gardening and cooking demonstrations using open hearth methods.

We need to add a few lines of copy here to introduce this section, and so that the B head is not the first thing immediately after an A head. Roz will supply some copy here. Something to introduce garden style, and so forth and so on and etc.

An heirloom garden can take any form. Heirloom vegetables and flowers can be intermingled with modern varieties or grown in a garden at their own. The following heirloom gardens illustrate many planting options.

The Pliny Freeman Garden

I went to Old Sturbridge Village, an outdoor museum of living history interpreting life in New England during the fifty years after the Revolution, on a classic bright, crisp Massachusetts autumn day. By happy accident, I met Christie White, the training interpreter for horticulture at the village, as she was dodging the mud puddles, clad in her brogans and bonnet. Someone pointed her out as the person who oversaw the vegetable gardens. I introduced myself, and immediately we were comparing notes on Indian flint corn and old 'Case Knife' beans. I soon discovered that Christie was well on her way to seeing that the village vegetable gardens were filled with the same varieties that were grown in the 1830s. Thus the gardens would be as true to the spirit of this New England village as the saltbox houses.

Christie's vast experience with heirlooms made her my prime resource for information on heirloom gardening in a historical context. When I interviewed her at Old Sturbridge Village,

I found her perspective on these vegetables and their growers to be quite different from that of most other heirloom gardeners. Others grow heirlooms for their taste or to preserve endangered seeds, but Christie was primarily concerned with the larger historical setting of heirlooms. Christie was also fascinated by the lives of the gardeners who tilled the soil in the 1830s. The extent of her absorption didn't really become clear, though, until I began transcribing my notes and noticed her consistent, eerie use of the present tense to refer to things that happened 170 years ago.

Christie led me to a re-created garden that is portrayed as that of a middle-class 1830s farmer by the name of Pliny Freeman. As was typical of the times, Mr. Freeman had a kitchen garden adjacent to his house in addition to the farm that provided grain, meat, and cider for the family. The kitchen garden, which covers about a quarter of an acre, would have been tended by his wife and children.

Christie had the garden maintained as closely as possible to the way it would have been in the early nineteenth century—dressed with manure and wood ashes, with crops rotated annually. The varieties, except for the cucumbers, are relatively maintenance-free, thus making them a good choice for modern New England gardeners. Christie obtained most of the seeds for the Freeman garden from Shumway's and Landreth seed companies.

As Christie explained to me about gardening as an exercise in history, "When we plan the gardens at the village, we allot certain portions of the garden based on what we think the people emphasized in their diet, so that much of the garden space is given over to vegetables that store well—carrots, beets, and turnips, for instance. There is a generous planting of beans and peas too. We have receipts [recipes] for them. In contrast, less space is given to lettuce, for example. A farmer like Mr. Freeman probably grew only a few types of lettuce—cos, a romaine type—and a mustard, but he supplemented these greens with easily gathered wild dandelions. As was customary, wild greens supplemented the few greens people grew in their gardens. Summer squash is grown at the Freeman house, and we don't preserve that in any way; but we might have three hills of summer squash to seven or eight hills of winter squash of various types, and

pumpkins are grown right in with the field corn for winter vegetable use.

"In the Freeman garden, some vegetables interest our visitors because they're unfamiliar. In particular, we grow 'Boston Marrow,' a good winter-keeping squash. It's very large, dramatic, and scarlet orange in color. It has sweet orange flesh that is very like pumpkin in flavor. What fall visitors also notice is that the 'Early Blood-Red Turnip Beet' and the 'Long Orange' carrot are generally much bigger and much more variable in size and shape than supermarket varieties. The large beet varieties grow to five inches across without becoming woody or unpleasant, because they were designed not only to be eaten fresh but also to be stored in the root cellar. The root vegetables really have to be large before they'll store well. Small, very thin carrots and

tiny beets tend to shrivel and wither in storage.

"We grow cabbages with storage in mind. 'Late Flat Dutch' and 'Mammoth Red Rock' cabbage both form very firm, tight heads. We store them by hanging them upside down in a root cellar or we bury them in an outside pit, or grave, as it was sometimes called.

"We also grow peas in the Freeman garden. Peas are an example of a vegetable that has been modified so much in recent years that it's very hard to obtain authentic varieties from 1830. We did obtain an old variety called 'Early Alaska,' as well as 'Prince Albert,' but for our tall-growing peas, until recently we had to grow a variety called 'Tall Telephone.' Obviously, with a name like 'Telephone,' this pea doesn't go back to 1830, but it is a late-

nineteenth-century variety resembling tall vining varieties cultivated earlier in the century. 'Tall Telephone' requires staking on pea brush—dead prunings of shrubs or trees—used to support peas.

"We also grow parsnips. Many of the visitors have never heard of them, but parsnips were very common in the 1830s. They store so well that we can leave them in garden rows over the winter and dig them up in March for a very sweet, delicious vegetable.

"Our bean, which we grow primarily for use as a shell bean, is the 'True Cranberry.' The shelled bean is as red as a cranberry. People visiting us aren't familiar with the traditional practice of leaving pole beans on the vine to mature in the pod for threshing, shelling out, and using as a dry bean. Accustomed only to eating beans fresh, they're often critical of our pole beans when they see them overmature. It's very common to hear a visitor comment, 'You should have picked your beans two weeks ago.' Then we have to explain that people in the 1830s, if they were growing a bean primarily for storage, would pick some of those beans in the very young, tender stage for immediate cooking but would leave most of the crop in the garden to mature for threshing so they could have beans over the winter.

"In addition to the vegetables, there are a few culinary herbs growing in the Freeman garden: horseradish, sage, basil, parsley, marjoram, chives, mint, dill, and summer savory. Some were eaten fresh, and others were dried. Unusual for today's gardens are the

hops that were grown to preserve a yeast culture.

"Many of our visitors remark on how their own gardens differ from those generally grown in the last century. The modern garden is designed for fresh eating in the summer; and if the time, space, and surplus vegetables are available, the gardener will put

Village are planted and interpreted to the public every year. Christie is doing more behind-the-scenes work these days, but with a little luck, you might run into her if you go for a visit. In speaking with her, I felt as if an important piece of my heirloom vegetable puzzle had slipped smoothly into place.

The Blüm Heirloom Garden

No one could be blasé traveling to Jan Blüm's garden. To get there, I drove northward out of Boise, Idaho, gaining altitude as I went. The highway straddles the famous Snake River Canyon, and as I continued northward I could see dry grassland and scrub for miles. The region looks so untamed, I couldn't help wondering how anyone could garden out there. But then I came into a lush garden filled with leafy vegetables and bright flowers. Butterflies and birds flitted about, completing the idyllic picture.

This is the home of Seeds Blüm, a mail-order seed company. Now, there are seed companies, and then there are seed companies. Some are exceedingly businesslike, with catalogs filled with color photos, but visiting them turns up a suite of offices with nary a plant in sight. Jan's catalog is black-and-white, but there is plenty of color in the huge vegetable garden that surrounds the office.

Blüm is very concerned about the erosion of the gene pool and directs much of her energy toward saving such varieties as the 'Super Italian Paste' tomato and 'Moon and Stars' watermelon. She actively searches out

aside some things for winter. In the nineteenth century the family garden was grown primarily for a year-round supply of vegetables; the fresh vegetables and greens of the summer months were a bonus to enjoy."

You can visit Old Sturbridge Village and see the Freeman garden and the other historical gardens as well as

attend their many events throughout the year—from herb classes to pressing apples for cider. For visitors passionate about heirloom vegetables one of the high points of the year is the annual event called "An Early Nineteenth-Century Agricultural Fair" celebrated in late September.

The gardens at Old Sturbridge

varieties on the brink of extinction and adds the gardening information she turns up to her catalog. "A great part of my satisfaction," she told me, "comes from people writing to say, for instance, that they haven't seen the 'Moon and Stars' watermelon since the 1930s. Or, 'I've kept thirty varieties of such and such alive for many years. Are you interested in having the seeds?'"

Having experienced Jan's grand enthusiasm for heirlooms, I knew she would be great as a prototype heirloom gardener. I asked Jan and her partner, Karla Prabucki, to create an heirloom garden; when I arrived to photograph it, it far exceeded my expectations. It overflowed with unusual and historically rich varieties of vegetables.

To begin our chat that day, I asked Jan to explain what she had in mind when she put the garden together. "I had a vast bank to pull from; but I had limited space. I wanted to feature old varieties of common vegetables—for instance, 'Red Lazy Wife' bean. That name implies history! I also chose German-Russian varieties from the Volga River area of Russia, where my mother's people came from. In the early 1800s there was a major flow of German people to settle the Volga area. This migration was reflected later in the gardens of immigrant families in this country. Consider the 'Moon and Stars' watermelon, for example. Most of Germany would have been too cold for watermelons, so this was probably originally a Russian variety that the Germans adopted. Watermelons became integrated into German cuisine, and watermelon pickles are now a tradition in German-American communities."

Another German variety Jan included in the garden was 'Ragged Jack' kale, also known as 'Red Russian' kale, one of Jan's favorite vegetables, as it is both tasty and beautiful, with its scalloped oaklike leaves and purple-colored veins. In its immature stage, it is also the best raw kale for salads. Jan also grew 'Rattailed' (also known as 'Rat's Tail') radish, which differs from most other radishes in that its roots are inedible. It is prized for its foot-long seed pods, which can be pickled, used raw in salads (sparingly), or cut up like green beans in stir-fries.

The vegetable border (*left*) at Seeds Blum is filled with 'Black-seeded Simpson' lettuces, bread seed poppies, 'Ragged Jack' kale, and sea kale—an old-time favorite pot herb.

In addition to the German-Russian varieties, Jan couldn't resist including some of her personal favorites: 'Blue Podded' peas, which have purple pods and flowers, and 'Red Lazy Wife' pole beans with their large, lush vines. The name supposedly refers to the beans' being relatively stringless. She also planted the 'Rough Vif d'Etampes' pumpkin. Originally from France, this squat, cheese-type pumpkin (so named because it looks like a wheel of cheese), eighteen inches wide and eight inches tall, is deep reddish orange, deeply fluted, and looks like the pumpkin for Cinderella's carriage.

During my visit Jan pointed out many plants—carrots, some lettuce plants, and three different kinds of chives—that were going to seed. As she said, "In the era this garden repre-

sents, there were, of course, few seed companies or produce markets. People were dependent upon the garden, and at any given time during the growing season there would be seedlings filling in, produce ready for harvesting, and seed heads forming for next year's seeds. These seed heads are a bonus; in addition to producing seeds, the extra heads can be used in all their different stages. Fresh carrot blossoms are long-lived, white, and lacy— excellent for flower arrangements and attracting beneficial insects." She noted that other seed heads used for arrangements include those of orach, bread-seed poppies, chives, elephant garlic, and leeks. "Sometimes," Jan concluded, "our modern gardens can seem sterile and one-dimensional in comparison."

Jan explained that not just heirloom vegetable varieties but also old, open-pollinated flower varieties, are endangered. In Jan's garden old varieties of red dianthus surrounded the ruby chard, and the hollyhocks were in bloom—the graceful single white ones called 'Tomb of Jesus'—as was another old-timer, 'Love-Lies-Bleeding' amaranth, with its long, "pink chenille" tassels. The flowers softened the look of the vegetable beds and, to the untrained eye, made them appear to be part of a lovely front-yard cottage garden.

The entry-way flower/vegetable bed (*above*) at Seeds Blum is planted with ruby chard, chives that have gone to seed, borage, and red dianthus. The bed to the left contains 'Blue Podded' peas, red orach, and serpent garlic.

Kent Whealy

K ent Whealy is director of the Seed Savers Exchange, an organization devoted to saving endangered open-pollinated varieties of vegetables. More than 1,000 members offer heirloom vegetable seeds through Seed Savers publications and help keep alive a gene pool of such unusual vegetables as 'Montezuma Red' beans and 'Afghani Purple' carrots. Seed Savers operates Heritage Farm in Decorah, Iowa, which maintains more than 18,000 varieties of heirloom vegetables. Kent, who has a degree in journalism, has com-

piled the *Garden Seed Inventory* (now in its fifth edition), a book listing and describing nearly 6,000 open-pollinated vegetable varieties sold by 240 companies in North America.

When I asked Kent to share some of his experiences with heirlooms, he first told me about the 'Moon and Stars' watermelon. This intriguing pink-fleshed watermelon is similar to many dark green ones but is covered with many small yellow spots, or "stars" and usually a large yellow spot, or "moon," which can be as large as four inches wide.

Kent said that exchange members had tried for about five years to find the 'Moon and Stars' watermelon through their network. Then in 1981, "we were living in Missouri and I did a television spot about the Seed Savers. After it aired, I got a call from Merle Van Doran, who told me he had 'Moon and Stars' and asked if I wanted some seed. I went to his farm, by chance only fifty miles away, and he had a whole field of the melons."

Kent talked, too, about the 'Cherokee' bean. Not all our heirloom varieties came from Europe, Africa, or Asia; many are native.

Kent Whealy (*above*) is the director of the Seed Saver's Exchange, an organization of seed savers devoted to saving an endangered vegetable gene pool.

tomatoes he has grown, this is one of the best. It's a large, meaty, pink tomato that's incredibly flavorful. Kent doesn't know where the name came from, only that the seeds came from the late Ben Quisenberry, who ran a company called Big Tomato Gardens, which offered tomato seeds for thirty years.

Kent also mentioned an especially sweet white corn. "It's so sweet," he said, "you can't dry it for seed on the plant, or it will mold. It's called 'Aunt Mary's' sweet corn." According to Kent, a fellow named Berkowitz visited his aunt Mary in Ohio in

According to Kent, "there was an old fellow, recently deceased, named Dr. John Wyche, a dentist of Cherokee descent from Hugo, Oklahoma. Dr. Wyche's people had traveled on the Trail of Tears, an Indian death march [the forced relocation of the Cherokees from their native lands in the southeastern states to Oklahoma], in 1838. He gave me several varieties of seeds that his people had carried [on the march; one we call the 'Cherokee' bean or the 'Cherokee Trail of Tears' bean, which is a snap bean. The seeds are black, and the pods are very long and purple and grow on vigorous climbing vines."

Then there's the tomato called 'Stump of the World.' Kent thinks that of the 510 varieties of

the 1930s, became enamored with her corn, and obtained some seeds from her. Two of Berkowitz's friends, W. W. Williams and his father, helped him produce the seeds. Forty years later Williams gave the seeds to Kent. As Kent said, "When someone like Williams gives me the seeds of something he's kept pure for forty years, I feel it's a gift from the past and I have an obligation to keep it going."

The 'Old Time Tennessee' muskmelon is another heirloom that Kent likes. He said it grows larger than a basketball and is unusual because, instead of being smooth, the rind has very deep creases. The way it grows is amazing: at first, it's very long and creased, like a deflated football; then, as it grows, it balloons and fills out.

According to Kent, "It's so very sweet and aromatic, you could find it in the dark."

Anyone interested in joining Kent and other seed savers can send for a free color catalog detailing the projects and publications of the Seed Savers Exchange (see Resources, page 102). Realize, though, that you are not merely sending for a seed catalog. The *Seed Savers Yearbook* offers 11,000 heirloom varieties. As a member, you have access to this incredible collection of wonderful vegetables and fruits that are not commercially available—but that's simply a benefit of what Kent refers to as "saving the sparks of life that feed us all."

'Grandpa Ott's' morning glories (*above*) bedeck the side of the Seed Savers barn. The teepees are covered with heirloom bean varieties. The garden at the Seed Savers in Decorah, Iowa (*right*) is filled with hundreds of open-pollinated varieties of vegetables. Different selections are grown out each year and the seeds cataloged and saved. The many 'cages' are to protect the different vegetables from cross-pollination by bees, thus contaminating the gene pool.

an encyclopedia of heirloom vegetables

The following entries describe how to grow and prepare heirloom vegetables, the majority of which have been in cultivation at least one hundred years. In the cooking sections, I have concentrated on Native American cooking methods and those used during Colonial times and the early nineteen century. See Appendices A and B (pages 90–101) for information on soil preparation, mulching, composting, and pests and diseases.

Whenever possible, the year that the variety was introduced to this country is given. Most of the varieties are either European or Native American heirlooms, as it was these cultures that had the most influence on early American gardening and cooking. For detailed information on the historical back-

ground of heirloom varieties, see William Woys Weaver's magnificent book, *Heirloom Vegetable Gardening*. For more information on the varieties, including nursery sources, consult Sue Stickland's *Heirloom Vegetables*.

When you buy or trade heirloom seeds be aware that over the years the same variety may have been spelled in

a number or ways or may have been renamed altogether (often by seed companies who want it to look like they have a new variety). For example, 'Kentucky Wonder' and 'Old Homestead' beans are the same entity. Confusion is also caused when one seed company calls a French variety by its French name while another gives it its English name, as in 'Marvel of Four Seasons' and 'Merveille des Quatre Saisons' lettuce. Where possible, I have given the most common alternative names in parenthesis after the variety name. For more information on which variety is which, consult the fifth edition of The Seed Savers' *Garden Seed Inventory*.

A harvest (*left*) from the Seed Savers garden includes corn, pole snap beans, and old-fashioned green-shouldered tomatoes.

AMARANTH

Amaranthus hypochondriacus,
A. tricolor, A. cruentus,
A gangeticus.

AMARANTH, A VALUABLE STAPLE of the Aztecs and Southwestern tribes in ancient times, is finally being rediscovered. Some varieties are grown for their leaves; others produce edible seeds or grain.

How to grow: Amaranth glories in warm weather. Start amaranth seedlings after any danger of frost has passed. Plant seeds ⅛ inch deep, 4 inches apart, in full sun, in rich, well-drained soil. Keep seedlings fairly moist and thin to 1 foot. Generally, amaranth grows with great enthusiasm. The leaf types grow to 2 feet, some of the grain varieties to 6 feet. Cucumber beetles are occasionally a problem. Harvest the leaf types when they are quite young. Harvest the grain types after the first frost in the North; in mild-winter areas, wait until

the heads begin to drop their seeds. Cut the tops and lay them on a tarp in the sun to dry for about a week; protect them against rain and heavy dew. Thresh the grain by laying the heads on sheets and doing the "tennis shoe twist"—standing on the heads and twisting and dancing on them—to knock the seeds free. Use an electric fan to separate the seeds from the lighter chaff as you pour them into a container.

Varieties
Grain Amaranths
'Golden Giant': 100 to 150 days, 6-foot-tall annual grown for its white grain and beautiful golden stems and seed heads, high yielding, leaves are also edible
'Hopi Red Dye' ('Komo'): 100 to 120 days, 5- to 6-foot-tall, reddish purple plant traditionally used by the Hopi as a food dye, both the black seeds and young leaves are edible

Leaf Amaranths
'Joseph's Coat': 70 days, a spectacular

Amaranth varities (*from left*): Grain amaranths, 'Joseph's Coat' amaranth, and 'Calaloo' (or Chinese spinach) amaranth

tricolor variety—red, cream, and green leaves, originally from India; leaf type, for garnishing
'Merah': 75 to 80 days, crinkled bicolored green-and-red leaves

How to prepare: Select young, tender leaves and shoots to use raw in salads. Or use young leaves from the leaf-type varieties as a substitute for spinach. The nutritious leaves are high in calcium and iron.

Amaranth grain has a mild and nutty flavor and is higher in protein than other grains. Amaranth flour contains no gluten, so it must be combined with wheat flour to make risen breads. The seeds can be popped like popcorn; stir ½ cup of seeds in a hot frying pan for about 30 seconds or until they pop. Mix the popped seeds with honey to create a traditional Mexican confection called *alegria*. The seeds can also be ground and added to breads.

BEANS
Snap Beans (string beans)
Phaseolus vulgaris

Lima Beans
P. limensis var. *limenanus*

Runner Beans
P. coccineus

THE PEOPLES OF THE AMERICAS grew beans for thousands of years; explorers brought them back to Europe, where they became integrated into the cuisine, eventually becoming a staple in the Colonial diet.

How to grow: Most types of beans grow well in warm climates. Runner beans, however, produce best when the temperature stays below 80°F. Plant all beans after any danger of frost is past, in full sun, in soil with plenty of added organic matter. Sow the seeds of bush beans 1 inch deep in rows 18 inches apart. Thin seedlings to 2 inches apart. Pole beans need a strong trellis, put in place before planting, to climb on. Plant pole bean seeds 1 inch deep, 2 inches apart. Thin seedlings to 6 inches apart. If your soil is fairly fertile, no extra fertilizing is needed. If beans look pale midseason, fertilize with fish emulsion. They are best watered deeply and infrequently at the base of the plants.

Beans have their share of pests, including bean beetles, beanloopers, whiteflies, aphids, and cucumber beetles. Anthracnose and a number of leaf-spot diseases are most prevalent in humid climates.

Harvest snap beans when the seeds inside are still very small and the pods are tender. Make sure you pick all the young beans as they come along, or the plants stop producing. Harvest young runner bean pods for snap beans (the pods are usually larger than standard snap beans). Fresh shelling beans should be harvested when the pods fill out noticeably but before they get dry. If they get too mature, allow them to dry for winter use.

For dried beans in rainy climates, drape whole plants over a crude drying frame or store them in the garage. In a dry climate, let the pods dry completely in the garden and harvest the whole plant. Once the bean pods are completely dry, separate the seeds from the pods. For a small batch, just shell the beans by hand. For larger harvests, cut a 6-inch hole in the bottom corner of a burlap bag and tie it closed with string. Put the plants in the bag, hang the bag on a branch, and beat it with a stick to loosen the beans from the pods. When most of the beans are free, hold a pan under the hole, untie the string, empty the beans into the pan, and remove the chaff. Repeat the process as necessary.

Clean the beans from the chaff; when the beans are completely dry, store them in a dry place in a container that will keep out bugs. To prevent weevils, first put the jars in the freezer for twenty-four hours to kill the eggs.

Beans from the Seed Savers garden

Heirloom beans at Seed Savers

Varieties

Hundreds of varieties of heirloom beans are available. The Vermont Bean Seed Company carries a large selection, and Native Seed-SEARCH carries Native American varieties.

Snap Beans

'Blue Lake': 62 days, pole, 6- to 8-foot vigorous and productive plant, sweet-tasting green pods

'Cherokee Trail of Tears': 90 days, 8-foot pole, prolific, purple-tinged pod, snap or dry beans, tradition says it was carried on the Trail of Tears forced march by the Cherokees from Georgia to Oklahoma during the winter of 1838–1839

'Fin des Bagnols' ('Shoestring Bean'): 55 days, bush, 1880s, French heirloom filet, pick while very young, every 2 to 3 days

'Hoffer's Lazy Wife': pole, stringless green pod; German and Pennsylvania heirloom; named for its ease of preparation

'Hopi Purple String Beans': purple with black crescent-moon-shaped stripes; can be grown with little or no irrigation

'Kentucky Wonder' ('Old Homestead'): 68 days, pole, popular since the mid-1800s and is still great, plants are rust resistant

'Trionfo Violetto': 65 days, pole, stringless purple-podded Italian heirloom, vigorous vines, deep lavender flowers

Lima Beans

'Christmas' ('Large Speckled Calico'): 100 days, pole, vines to 10 feet, 1840s, nutty-tasting white seeds with maroon spots, high yields, does well in hot, humid weather

'Dr. Martins': 100 days, pole, vines to 10 feet, about 1935, developed by a dentist in Pennsylvania, 5-inch pods with two to four huge beans each, plant when soil is warm

'Jackson Wonder': 66 days, bush, 1888, developed by a Georgia farmer, small seeds buff with purple-black mottling, good fresh or dried; plants do well in North or South, hardy, drought tolerant

'King of the Garden': 95 days, pole, dark green 8-inch pods, rich, nutty-tasting beans, high yields

Runner Beans
(grown for snap, shell, or dry beans)

'Painted Lady': 100 days, vigorous vine, 1855, red and pinkish white bicolored flowers, pods to 12 inches, brown-and-white seeds

Scarlet Runner: perennial vine grown as an annual, red flowers, pods to 1 foot, prefers cooler climates

Shelling and Dry Beans

'Black Turtle': 90 days, bush, South American, from before 1806, shiny black beans, hardy disease- and heat-resistant plants

'Borlotto': 73 days, bush, Italian heirloom, colorful rose-and-cream pods, delicious creamy white beans with rosy speckles

'Genuine Cornfield Pole': 72 days,

originally from Mexico, long favored by Iroquois, can be planted among corn plants, 6-inch pods, 10- to 15-foot vines, heavy producer, pods can be eaten when young but they are best shelled fresh and dried

'Great Northern' ('Great Northern White'): 65 days for shelling beans, 95 for dry beans, bush, introduced in 1907 but originally obtained from Mandan tribe, white bean, often available in grocery stores

'Hidatsa Shield Figure': 90 days, pole, from Hidatsa Indians in North Dakota, large white bean with speckled tan "shield"

'Jacob's Cattle' ('Trout'): 85 to 95 days, bush, New England favorite, originally from the Passamaquoddy tribe, white seeds with maroon splotches, for shelling or dry, in baked beans keeps its shape

'Low's Champion': 90 days, bush, 1884, New England heirloom, strain of 'Dwarf Cranberry Bean', small deep-cranberry beans with white eyes

'New Mexico Bolitas': New Mexico heirloom, these light brown beans cook faster than pintos

'Santa Maria Pinquito': 75 to 90 days, vigorous semi-trailing vines, 1/3-inch long squared off pink beans, valued in California since the days of the early Spaniards, stays intact when cooked, great for baked beans and refried beans

'Soldier': 85 days, bush, well-known New England heirloom, slender, kidney-shaped, white seed marked with a "soldier" in yellow brown on the eye; does well in cool climates and in drought

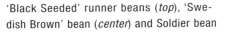

'Black Seeded' runner beans (*top*), 'Swedish Brown' bean (*center*) and Soldier bean

'Christmas' lima beans (*top*), 'Jacob's cattle' bean (*center*), 'Dr. Martin's' lima

'**Swedish Brown**': 85 days, bush, very hardy, plump, oval, brown beans with a dark eye rim; popular in Scandinavian-settled areas in the United States

'**Vermont Cranberry**': 75 days for shelling, 98 days for dry, pole; old northern New England variety, for all climates, round, deep maroon beans, a version of cranberry bean; some have speckled seeds, others have colorful pods

'**Yellow Eye**' ('**Maine Yellow Eye**'): 95 days, bush, hardy, traditional in New England, oval white bean with yellow eye; prolific, reliable, disease-resistant plant; takes less time to cook than most beans

How to prepare: Most of the old varieties of green beans have a string

down the side (hence the name string bean) that must be removed. String or puree them to serve as a side dish or make into soup.

Commenting on how early European settlers cooked beans, Debra Friedman said, "A lot of the old-time recipes for baked or boiled beans were very bland. Cooks might have boiled the beans and added some butter or parsley, or baked them with pepper and salt pork. But the type of baked beans with molasses that everybody is so fond of today had yet to appear. Most of the baked beans were a hardy side dish served at breakfast or dinner."

From left to right: Fava beans, 'Black Seeded Yellow Wax' beans,'Blue Lake' snap beans, 'King of the Garden' limas, and the speckled cranberry pods

BEETS
Beta vulgaris

A CLOSE RELATIVE OF CHARD, beets originated in Europe almost four thousand years ago. The ancient Greeks and Romans enjoyed both red and white beets. Yellow beets were popular for centuries. Early settlers to America appreciated the beet's keeping qualities and relied on them to provide food in early spring.

How to grow: Sow beet seeds directly in rich, well-drained soil in early spring or in the fall, in full sun. In mild climates beets can be grown most of the year. A soil pH of 7 seems best. Many gardeners agree that beets become sweeter with some chilling as they mature. They can take some frost. Plant the seeds 1/4 inch deep in wide rows or broadcast them over a 3-foot-wide bed. Beet seeds are a cluster of seeds; therefore, thinning is essential to prevent crowding. Thin modern beets to 3 inches apart and large keeper beets to 6 inches apart. Fertilize midseason with a balanced organic fertilizer and water evenly.

Occasionally, leaf miners tunnel through the leaves; control them with neem or floating row covers. A more common problem is cercospora, a fungus that thrives in humid conditions and leaves orange spots on the foliage. A rust fungus can also be a problem.

Harvest modern varieties when they are 3 inches or smaller. The large keeper beets (which will grow up to 6 inches across) are planted 90 days before your first expected frost. Mulch them, and they will winter over if temperatures aren't too cold. In severe climates the roots can be stored for up to four months in damp sand in a root cellar kept just above freezing.

Golden, white, and 'Chioggia' red and white beets

'Burpee's Golden' beets

'Chioggia,' 'Golden,' 'Bull's Blood', and
'Detroit Dark Red' beets

Keeper beets 'Lutz Green Leaf'

Varieties

'Albina Verduna' ('Show White'): 65
days, Dutch heirloom, pure white,
large and sweet, used to make white
beet sugar

'Chioggia': 50 days, Italian heirloom
known since the middle of the 1800s
in America, red on the outside,
white inside with red rings like
bull's-eyes

'Crosby's Egyptian': 50 to 60 days,
introduced in 1880, small dark red
bunching beet, early beet of choice,
has a rather flattened shape

'Cylindra' ('Formanova'): 60 days,
1880s, sweet dark red long
cylindrical-shaped beet, good for
slicing, keep the top of the root
covered with soil while growing

'Detroit Dark Red': 60 days, 1892,
U.S. heirloom and for years the
standard beet of commerce, popular
with home gardeners, uniform color
and shape

'Golden Beet': 60 days, before 1828,
European, sweet golden roots that
don't "bleed" so won't discolor salads and other dishes, low germination rate, so plant extra

**'Lutz Green Leaf' ('Winter Keeper,'
'Lutz Salad'):** 80 days, sweet and
tender even when 6 inches across,
reddish purple roots, great storage
beet; wonderful for roasting in coals

How to prepare: The "keeper" beets
take a little longer to cook but are still
the best for making borscht, pickling,

or baking. Debra Friedman recounts,
"Back in Colonial times, the tops were
used as well as the roots. The beets
themselves, with their fairly tough
skins, could be roasted as potatoes
might be—whole in the embers of the
fire." Today you can bake them in a
covered casserole to closely duplicate
this presentation (see page 86). Steam
the greens and serve them with butter.

28

CABBAGES
Broccoli, Sprouting Brassica
oleracea var. *italica*

Brussels Sprouts
B. oleracea var. *gemmifera*

Cabbage, Heading and Savoy
Brassica oleracea var. *capitata;*
B. o. var. *bullata*

Cauliflower
B. oleracea var. *botrytis*

Collards
B. oleracea var. *acephala*

Kale
B. oleracea var. *acephala*

CABBAGE IS THE PROGENITOR OF
many other vegetables, often called
cole crops: broccoli, cauliflower, collards, and kale. Brussels sprouts are
essentially tiny cabbages that pop out
along the length of the plant stem.
Broccolis are but the flowering stems
of plants that evolved from ancient
cabbages. Collards are large-leafed,
nonheading greens that are a cross
between cabbage and kale. Knowing
that all these vegetables are related is
important because related plants often
fall prey to the same pests and can
interbreed and so upset your seed-
saving efforts.

How to grow: Cole crops are best
grown as cool-season annuals. Collards
prefer cool weather but can do quite
well in hot weather too. All need full
sun, or light shade in hot climates.
Transplants of heirloom cabbage,

broccoli, and cauliflower are seldom
available from local nurseries. Start
seeds indoors eight weeks before your
last average frost date. (Plant cauliflower a little earlier, as it grows more
slowly.) Transplant seedlings into rich
soil filled with organic matter about
two weeks before the last average frost
date. Cabbage and broccoli seeds or
plants can also be planted in midsummer for a fall crop. Space small varieties of cabbage 1 foot apart and larger
ones 2 feet apart. Broccoli and cauliflower plants should be spaced 2 feet

apart. Cabbages tend to be top-heavy;
when transplanting, place them lower
in the soil—up to their first set of true
leaves (the first leaves after the seed
leaves). Start brussels sprouts about
four weeks before the last average frost
date and transplant them in a month.
Space the plants 2 feet apart. Kale and
collards can be started from seed in
early spring, but most gardeners start
them midsummer. Plant collard and
kale seeds $1/2$ inch deep, 1 inch apart,
and then thin seedlings to 18 inches
apart.

'Winningstädt' cabbage at Old Sturbridge
Village

'Long Island Improved' brussels sprouts

'Early Purple Sprouting' broccoli

'Early Jersey Wakefield' cabbage

Most cole family seedlings are heavy feeders, so add a balanced organic fertilizer: 1 cup worked into the soil around each plant at planting time. Side dress with blood meal or other organic nitrogen fertilizer worked into the soil a month after planting. Kale and collards need a bit less fertilizer. All cole crops need regular and even watering and a substantial mulch.

All cabbage family members are susceptible to the same pests and diseases, though kale and collards tend to have far fewer problems. Flea beetles, imported cabbageworm, cabbage root fly, and cutworms are potential problems. Prevent these pests with floating row covers. Rotate members of the cabbage family with other vegetable families to prevent diseases.

Harvest cabbages anytime after they have started to form a decent head but before they become so large that they split. Mature cabbages can take temperatures as low as 20°F. If you expect a hard freeze, harvest all your cabbages

and store them in a cool place. Harvest broccoli when the buds begin to swell but before they open. Once the primary head is harvested, many smaller heads form. If planted in late summer, broccoli will produce into fall and can withstand light frosts. Cauliflower heads need protection from the sun. Modern varieties have leaves that grow over the head, but most heirlooms need to have the leaves tied up around the head a few weeks before harvesting. Harvest cauliflower heads at the base when they are very full but before the curds (the partially developed flower heads) begin to separate.

Harvest brussels sprouts in the fall or winter, when frost improves their flavor. Toward the end of their development, cut off the growing tip of each plant and remove the leaves growing between the sprouts. This diverts the plant's remaining energy to developing the sprouts. If the plants are kept well mulched with straw, sprouts often develop and mature well into the win-

ter. Brussels sprouts mature up the stem, from the bottom to the top, so harvest a few at a time in that direction. Harvest them when they're no larger than 1 inch in diameter.

Harvest a few very young kale leaves at a time as they are needed for salads, or use mature kale leaves for cooked dishes. The flavor and color of kale improve after a frost, and kale winters over in most climates. In the very coldest areas, cover kale with floating row covers.

Harvest collard leaves while they are young. If harvested a few leaves at a time, collards produce over a long period. Like kale, collards are valuable as a fall crop since their flavor sweetens with frost.

Varieties
Broccoli

'Calabrese': 58 days, 1880s, Italian heirloom green sprouting broccoli with a long season of side shoots after main head is cut

Collards

Collection of kale

'Russian Red' kale

'**Early Purple Spouting**': 125 days, before 1835, 2 to 3 feet high, very hardy, purple-green leaves, purple flower buds

Brussels Sprouts

'**Bedford Fillbasket**': 85 to 100 days, large sprouts, good yields

'**Long Island Improved**': 90 to 100 days, 1890s, tight, closely formed sprouts, good yields, hardy old favorite

Savoy Cabbage

'**Chieftain Savoy**': 85 days, 1938 American heirloom, dark green leaves, mild flavor which improves with frost

Standard and Red Cabbages

'**Early Flat Dutch**'('**Stein's Drumhead**'): 1 foot across, 10 to 12 pounds, dense fine flesh, terrific for sauerkraut, tolerates heat fairly well

'**Early Jersey Wakefield**': 65 days,

1820s, English heirloom, green small conical-shaped heads with great flavor, good fall crop for mild climates, resistant to the disease yellows

'**Late Flat Dutch**': 110 days, brought to America before 1840 by European settlers, flattened heads 14 inches across; keeps well

'**Red Drumhead**': 1860s, purplish red very sweet heads, hardy, widely adaptable plant

'**Ruby Perfection**': 80 days, deep purple cabbage with great taste

'**Winningstädt**': first mentioned in 1864 in America, large, dense, conical heads great for sauerkraut and coleslaw

Cauliflower

'**Early Snowball**': 50 days, compact plants, 1888, does especially well in the midatlantic area, 6-inch-white heads, curd covered well by the wrapper leaves

'**Purple Cape**': 1834, purple heads turn green when cooked, hardy to

USDA Zone 6, popular in Europe, for seeds, contact Chiltern Seeds in England

Collards

'**Georgia Green**' ('**Georgia Southern**'): 70 days, before 1880, 3-foot-tall, upright plant, sweet blue green, tolerates poor soil and temperature extremes

'**Green Glaze**': 79 days, 1820, bright green smooth leaves, frost and heat resistant, highly resistant to pests such as cabbage looper and cabbageworm

Kale

'**Dwarf Green Curled**': 65 days, highly curled, light green leaves, plants to 18 inches

'**Lacinato**': 62 days, Italian heirloom, to 5 feet tall, unique dark blue green kale with thick crinkly leaves, wide temperature tolerance

'**Ragged Jack**' ('**Red Russian**', '**Russian Red**'): 55 days, heirloom, tender

31

frilly gray green leaves with red veins, young leaves good in salads, withstands summer heat

How to prepare: The old varieties of cabbages are usually dense and rot resistant, selected to be preserved in the root cellar. This also makes them perfect for making coleslaw, pickling, and making sauerkraut. The English settlers preferred pickled cabbage, a vinegar process; the Dutch and Germans chose to preserve cabbage as sauerkraut, a fermenting process. Both dishes had many variations. Spices and other vegetables were added to pickled cabbage, and sauerkraut could be cooked up with sausage, pork, potatoes, or other vegetables.

Cabbages were also used in soups, stuffed, and made into gratins. Often the boiled wedges would be served as part of a boiled dinner. Coleslaw or hot slaw were other favorites.

Brussels sprouts were another winter staple, boiled (probably overcooked by our standards) and served as a side dish with butter or cream and seasonings.

Cauliflower is a labor-intensive plant to grow, so it was considered a luxury. The heads were poached and served whole with considerable flourish.

Collard leaves were cooked as greens and served as a side dish or added to soup stocks, either alone or mixed with other greens, and often combined with pork.

I could find little information on how kale was cooked in early America; I can only assume it was boiled and served with butter, salt, and pepper like most other greens and used in soups.

Broccoli was not a well-known vegetable in early America, and its use was confined to Italian neighborhoods. It was probably prepared as it has been in southern Italy for centuries: boiled, then drained and reheated in olive oil with garlic and Parmesan cheese. It was not until the victory-garden era, when the U.S. government dispersed information on nutrition, that most Americans became aware of the virtues of broccoli, namely its flavor and high nutritional value.

CARROTS
Daucus carota, var. *sativus*

ANCIENT CARROTS CAME FROM Afghanistan, and their roots were mainly white, red, or purple. The familiar orange-colored carrots are relative newcomers, having been bred in Holland in the 1600s. The French refined the carrot in the 1800s.

How to grow: Carrots taste best and are easiest to grow in cool weather. Plant carrots in early spring as soon as your soil has warmed, or plant them as a fall crop. Cultivate and loosen the soil 1 foot deep to make room for the roots. Light soil is best, so gardeners with heavy soil should select stubby varieties. Sow seeds $1/2$ inch apart in rows or wide beds and keep the seed bed evenly moist. Thin to 2 inches apart. In most parts of the country, once sprouted, carrots are easy to grow. When the plants are about 3 inches tall, mulch with compost or side dress with fish emulsion.

Once the seedlings are up, protect them from snails and slugs. In the upper Midwest, the carrot fly maggot tunnels its way through carrots. Floating row covers and crop rotation help. Alternaria blight and cercospora blight can also be a problem.

Most modern carrot varieties are ready for harvesting when the carrots

'Red Suprex,' 'Early Scarlet Horn,' 'Long Orange,' 'Ox Heart,' and 'Belgian White' carrots

'Ox Heart,' 'Belgian White,' 'Long Orange,' and 'Red Suprex' carrots at Old Sturbridge Village with a carrot flower

are at least ¹/₂ inch across and have started to color. The optimal time to harvest them is within a month after they mature, less in very warm weather. Large heirloom carrots can grow to 4 inches across and still be tender. These will store in the ground for months. Harvest all carrots when the soil is moist, to reduce the risk of breaking off the roots in the ground. To prolong the fall harvest in cold climates, mulch plants well with 1 foot of dry straw and cover them with plastic that's weighted down with something heavy. Just spread the snow and mulch aside to harvest your carrots.

Varieties

'Belgium White' ('White Belgian'): 75 days, before 1863, 8 to 10 inches, white inside and out, flavor can become too strong in warm weather

'Danvers Half Long': 75 days, 1871 American heirloom, originated by market gardeners in Danvers, Massachusetts, bright orange, 6 to 8 inches long, great for most soil types

'Early Scarlet Horn': 65 to 70 days, oldest cultivated carrot, available since before 1610 and named for the Dutch town of Hoorn, short, 2 to 6 inches long, excellent flavor

'Oxheart' ('Guerande'): 73 to 80 days, 1884, a dense-textured short stubby carrot with good flavor, can grow to a pound, stores well in a root cellar

How to prepare: Enjoy the large storage varieties baked, steamed, and roasted in coals. All types of carrots were used in soups and stews, boiled and served cold in a salad, and pureed and made into a pie similar to pumpkin pie, which was usually served as part of the meal not as a dessert (see recipe, page 88). Debra Friedman reports that "In Colonial times, carrots were boiled, and probably overcooked by modern standards. People were very fond of cooked carrots cold as well. In fact, people of this period probably did not eat carrots raw."

'Improved Golden Bantam' corn (*above*); many grinding corns from the 'Seed Savers' garden (*below*)

CORN
(maize, Indian corn)

Dent Corn
Zea mays, var. *indentata*

Flint Corn
Z. m., var. *indurata*

Popcorn
Z. m., var. *everta*

Soft Corn
Z. m., var. *amylacea*

Sweet Corn
Z. m., var. *saccharata*

LONG BEFORE EUROPEAN explorers and settlers came to the New World, Native Americans cultivated a wide variety of corn. To them, corn—often called Sacred Mother—was considered a gift from the gods.

What pleasure awaits those who go beyond tasting corn only for its sweetness. Corn has many more dimensions. In simple terms, sweet corn is the one that bears those luscious ears we smother with butter; dent, flint, and soft (flour) corns are primarily ground into corn meal or corn flour. Dent varieties are also roasted or ground and popped.

How to grow: Requiring both summer heat and full sun, corn is generally planted from seeds sown directly in the garden. Corn pollen is transferred by the wind, from the male flower (the tassel) onto the pistil of the female flower (the silk). If corn is planted in long single rows, the silks won't be well pollinated. Instead plant corn in a block of shorter multiple rows, at least four rows deep. Plant seeds in rich soil, 1 inch deep, 4 inches apart, with 3 feet between rows. Or plant corn in hills of four plants each, with 3 feet between hills and 4 feet between rows. In all cases, thin corn seedlings to 1 foot apart.

The hill method of planting corn, with squash plants between the hills and pole beans growing up the corn stalks, is the traditional method for some Native American cultures. To duplicate the process, choose tall varieties of corn, long vining squashes, and 'Cornfield' beans. Plant the corn two weeks before the beans and squash.

Sweet corn is a heavy feeder and needs lots of nitrogen throughout the season. Grinding corns are usually lighter feeders and more drought tolerant. With all corn, however, water carefully as it develops, especially at tasseling time (when the flower stalks produce pollen), to guard against poorly filled out ears.

The most common insect pest, corn earworm, can be smothered by a bit of mineral oil squirted into the ear just as the silk begins to dry; or apply *Bacillus thuringiensis* to the plant. Other insect pests include corn borers, southern corn rootworms, corn flea beetles, and seed corn maggots. Birds can steal the seeds out of the ground, so use floating row covers. The most common corn diseases are Stewart's bacterial wilt, root rot, corn smut, and southern corn leaf blight.

Sweet corn is ready to eat when the silks are dry and brown and the ears are well filled out. Test for ripeness by puncturing a few kernels with a fin-

gernail. Unripe kernels squirt a watery liquid, ripe ones a milky juice. Since heirloom sweet corns begin to lose their sweetness as soon as they are picked, harvest the ears as close to cooking time as possible.

Grinding corns and popcorn should be left on the plant until the kernels are dry. If the weather is very wet, cut the stalks after the husks begin to turn brown; store them in a dry place. When the corn is completely dry—which can take weeks—husk the ears and store them in a dry place, or remove the kernels and store them in sealed jars.

Varieties
Grinding Corns

'Bloody Butcher': 100 days, 1845, dent corn, roast ears when it's young, grind when mature, red kernels make pink corn meal, large ears, plants grow to 12 feet

'Hopi Blue' ('Sakwa-pu'): 90 days, flour corn with blue kernels, old Hopi variety used ceremonially to make blue piki bread, also makes great blue tortillas, drought tolerant

'Northstine Dent': 100 days, 7-foot stalks, 8-inch ears, early, does well in short-season areas, yellow grinding corn, makes great polenta

'Reid's Yellow Dent': 110 days, 7-foot stalks, 9-inch ears, heirloom yellow dent grinding corn adapted to Southern conditions

'Squaw Corn': 105 days, flint corn with red, yellow, orange, and blue kernels, large ornamental ears

'Bloody Butcher' corn growing in my garden (*above*), and a close-up of the corn kernels (*below*)

Seed corn 'Virginia Gourd' at Accoceek

Popcorn

'Strawberry': 80 to 110 days, ears are
dark red, 2 inches long, strawberry-
shaped; plants 5 feet tall; resistant to
corn earworm

Sweet Corns

Heirloom sweet corns are not as sweet
as the modern super sweets, but for
those of us who seek out a great corn
flavor—these babies have it!

'Country Gentleman' ('Shoe-Peg'): 80
to 100 days, 1891, white corn, cobs
to 8 inches, kernels grow every
which way and are long thin and
crunchy, good "corny" taste, resistant to Stewart's wilt

'Golden Bantam': 70 to 83 days, 1902,
the old standard for sweet corn,
sweet yellow kernels, cobs 6 inches
long; 'Improved Golden Bantam'
and 'Early Golden Bantam' are
related

'Howling Mob': 80 to 85 days, early
white corn, 9-inch ears, 1905 by C.
D. Keller of Ohio, according to him
this corn is so good that when he
went to market he was met by a
mob of buyers

How to prepare: Historically, corn
was critical to the diet of the peoples of
the New World. The majority was
grown for winter food. In New
England wheat did not grow well; to
quote Sarah Emery, who grew up in
the late 1700s in Massachusetts,
"Indian meal (corn meal) and rye,
especially rye, were the staples for daily
use in most households. . . . Wheat
flour was somewhat a luxury." Dent,
flint, and flour corns were primarily
ground as cornmeal or corn flour.
Sweet corn, also called green corn, was
usually eaten steamed fresh on the cob,
or the husks were soaked in water and
roasted whole over coals. The kernels
were also scraped or cut off the cob
and creamed, made into relishes,
mixed with other summer treats like

summer squash and fresh beans, and
used in chowders and soups, fritters,
green corn pudding, and succotash.
Native Americans also roasted sweet
corn over coals until it was dry enough
for storage. The dry, shriveled sweet
corn, plus dry beans, was then reconstituted for a chewy winter version of
succotash or used in stews.

Green (young and fairly sweet) dent
corn was primarily roasted in coals.
Mature dent corn was dried and
ground for corn bread, yeast breads,
and flapjacks. Dent and many of the
flint corns were also used in related
dishes, namely cornmeal mush (the
Italians have used a variation for
centuries, polenta); spoon bread, a
Southern variation with eggs, leaven-
ing, and flavorings; and New England
Indian pudding made with milk,
molasses, and spices. Dent corn was
also treated with lye before it was
made into hominy grits. Flint corn, as
the name suggests, is hard and was
ground and used for brown bread,
could be treated with lye and ground
for making grits and hominy, or was
toasted in a dry frying pan until slightly golden and ground for corn bread.
Flour corns are much softer, are primarily grown in the Southwest, and
have historically been ground and
used in tortillas, piki bread, and soups
and stews.

For centuries, corn was ground on
grinding stones. Today you can grind
dry corn in a grain mill—for example,
KitchenAid makes an attachment to fit
its stand mixers. Flour and dent corns
are easier to grind than flint and popcorns.

CUCUMBERS
Cucumis sativus, C. anguria

CUCUMBERS ARE AN ANCIENT vegetable that originated in India. The Chinese and Japanese had developed long varieties by the seventh century B.C., and cucumbers were also known to the ancient Greeks and Romans. Cucumbers were brought to America from Europe early on, and the settlers considered them indigestible when eaten raw.

How to grow: Cucumbers are warm-season annuals and tolerate no frost. They are usually grown in hills of three plants or planted 1 foot apart in rows. Plant the seeds when the soil and weather are warm, about 1 inch deep, 6 seeds to a hill, or 6 inches apart in rows. Thin later to 2 plants per hill or 2 feet apart in rows. Cucumbers grow on vines that need support; put trellises in place at the time of planting.

Cucumbers need rich, humus-filled soil and ample water during the growing season. Work bonemeal and blood meal into the soil before planting. If plants are pale, apply fish emulsion and kelp meal. Young cucumber plants are susceptible to cutworms and snails, and striped and spotted cucumber can destroy young vines. These insects also carry serious diseases.

Powdery mildew is a common problem, particularly late in the season. More serious diseases are mosaic virus, scab, and anthracnose. Pull up affected plants, as there is no cure for these conditions.

Harvest cucumbers when they are young and firm but filled out. Harvest

'White' cucumber (*top*); 'Armenian' cucumber (*bottom*)

them regularly and pick off all over-ripe or damaged fruit, or plants will stop production.

Varieties

'Armenian' ('Yard Long'): 60 to 65 days, long slender fruit, mild flavor, excellent for slicing

'Lemon': 60 to 65 days, pre-1900s, East Indian heirloom, round yellow fruit for slicing, mild flavor, pick when about the size of a lime but before fruit turns very yellow, drought and rust resistant

'West Indian Gherkin' ('West India Burr Gherkin'): 60 days, 1793, heavy producer of 3-inch fruits for pickling, superb flavor, not useful as slicing cucumber

'White': 60 days, crisp white slicing cucumber, probably a strain of 'White Wonder,' pick when 5 inches long and ivory white

How to prepare: In Colonial America cucumbers were popularly served as pickles, since pickling was a way of preserving them for the winter. In summer fresh cucumbers were coated with flour, fried in butter, and served for breakfast. Cucumbers might also be simmered awhile, split in half and stuffed with bread crumbs and seasonings, and baked. They were also stewed in butter with seasonings (and sometimes onions) and served as a side dish.

LETTUCE
(head, romaine/cos, and leaf)
Lactuca sativa

THE FABULOUS ARRAY OF lettuces are among our most ancient vegetables, having been cultivated by ancient Egyptians, Greeks, and Romans.

How to grow: Lettuce is a cool-season annual crop that can be grown in most areas of the country. Most varieties go to seed or become bitter rapidly once the hot weather arrives. In warm weather lettuce grows better with afternoon or filtered shade. In mild-winter areas lettuce grows through the winter.

Lettuce prefers soil high in organic matter. It needs regular moisture and profits from light feedings of fish emulsion or fish meal fertilizer every few weeks. Sow seeds 1/8 inch deep outdoors, start seeds indoors in flats, or buy transplants. You can start lettuce outside as soon as you can work the soil in the spring. Plant seeds 2 inches apart, 1/8 inch deep. Keep seed beds uniformly moist until seedlings appear. Thin seedlings to between 6 and 12 inches apart, depending on the variety. Failure to thin seedlings can result in disease problems.

Until they get fairly good sized, protect seedlings from birds, slugs, snails, and aphids with floating row covers and hand picking. Botrytis, a gray mold-fungus disease, can cause the plants to rot off at the base. Downy mildew, another fungus, causes older leaves to get whitish patches that eventually kill the plant.

'Iceberg' lettuce

Harvest lettuce at any stage. If possible, harvest during the cool of the day. Leaf lettuces can be harvested one leaf at a time or in their entirety. Heading lettuces are generally harvested by cutting off the head at the soil line.

Seed saving: When the yellow flowers have dried to stalks with feathery white seed heads, remove the seeds by shaking them into an open container, in which they can continue to dry indoors for about a week. You will lose some of the seeds, as they shatter from the pods very easily.

Lettuces are mostly self-pollinated, so you can grow several varieties for seed saving, but some crossing does occur, both from one variety to another and with wild lettuce, sometimes known as prickly lettuce. To keep crossing to a minimum, separate different varieties by 20 feet and eliminate wild lettuce plants.

Varieties
'Black-Seeded Simpson': 45 days, 1870s, popular American heirloom, light green crinkly leaf lettuce, one of the earliest lettuces, sensitive to weather extremes and prone to rot at its base

'Iceberg': 70 days, 1894, heirloom for the home garden, superior to the supermarket variety, fairly large tight heads, mosaic resistant and heat tolerant

'Limestone Bibb' ('Bibb,' 'Limestone'): 55 days, 1850, from Kentucky, small head lettuce with crispy leaves, especially good for the North, bolts readily in hot weather

'Black-Seeded Simpson' lettuce

'Tom Thumb' lettuce

'Paris Island' romaine lettuce

'Oak Leaf': 60 days, popular since 1800s or earlier, medium green, deeply lobed leaves, heat tolerant

'Paris Cos White': 80 days, pre-1868, large romaine type with medium green leaves, good for fall and mild winters

'Tom Thumb': 65 days, English heirloom, solid butterheads about the size of tennis balls, can be served whole as individual salads

'White Boston': 60 days, American heirloom, small loose heads of tender light green leaves, one of our first "gourmet" lettuces

How to prepare: In ancient Rome young lettuce leaves were popular as a first-course salad; older leaves were cooked and served with oil and vinegar. For centuries raw lettuce has been used as the basis of a salad, either by itself or with other greens. As American Fearing Burr stated in 1865, "Lettuce is well known as one of the best of all salad plants. . . . It is also eaten with sugar and vinegar; and some prefer it with vinegar alone." He also stated that lettuce is indispensable in lobster and chicken salads. Lettuces such as 'Loos Tennisball' and 'Tom Thumb' were pickled and seasoned with cloves in the 1600s and 1700s for winter use. Lettuces have also been cooked and included in soups; lettuce braised in butter is still popular in France today.

'Oak Leaf' lettuce with Ben Slotnick

MELONS

Canteloupe *(muskmelon)*
Cucumis melo var. *reticulatus*

Honeydew
C. melo var. *inodorus*

Watermelon
Citrullus lanatus

MELONS ORIGINATED IN THE HEAT of West Africa, but most of the melons we know today were developed in Central Asia and brought here in the 1800s by immigrants. Much of Europe was too cool to grow good melons except under glass, but the mid-Atlantic region of the United States is perfect.

How to grow: For general growing information on melons, see the entry on cucumbers on page 37. Melons are more sensitive to cool conditions than cucumbers are, so in coolsummer areas use a black-plastic mulch to raise the soil temperature. Reduce watering toward harvest; too much water at that time results in insipid fruit and split melons.

'Turkey', 'Bidwell' and 'Hopi' cantaloupe (*top*), 'Moon and Star' watermelon (*above*), and watermelon slices from the many varieties at the Seed Savers (*below*)

Cantaloupe is ready to harvest when its netting, the raised markings on the skin, has turned from green to tan, the fruit smells rich and fragrant, and it detaches easily from the stem. Honeydews are ready when their rind shows hints of yellow. Watermelon is ripe when the fruit's surface skin is dull, tough, and difficult to puncture with your fingernail; the bottom of the melon has passed through green to yellow; and the tendrils on the stem near the fruit are brown.

Varieties

Sand Hill Preservation Center has a very large selection of melons.

Cantaloupe and Honeydew

'Hale's Best': 75 to 88 days, pre-1923, 2- to 3-pound salmon-fleshed cantaloupe with sweet flavor, drought and powdery mildew resistant

'Jenny Lind': 70 to 85 days, pre-1846, turban shaped, to 2 pounds, green melons with light green sweet juicy flesh

'Old Time Tennessee': 90 days, old-time favorite, football-shaped, salmon-colored cantaloupe, outstanding flavor if picked at the peak of ripeness, very aromatic, fragile, so should be eaten quickly after harvest

'Turkey': 90 days, very old Southern variety, large football-shaped, honeydew type melon, 8 to 10 pounds or larger with good flavor

Watermelon

'Blackstone': 91 days, dark green, pale red flesh, thick rind suitable for pickling

'Ice Cream': 82 days, 1871 or before, very light green, to 25 pounds, pink flesh, white-fleshed, white-seeded 'Ice Cream' is an even older variety, but seeds are hard to find

'Moon and Stars' ('Sun, Moon, and Stars'): 95 to 105 days, before 1910, to 30 pounds, pinkish red flesh with fine flavor, black seeds, leaves and green rind are covered with gold splotches (moons) and smaller gold speckles (stars)

'Rattlesnake' ('Southern Rattlesnake,' 'Gypsy Oblong'): 90 days, 1830s, to 40 pounds, *the* watermelon for folks who grew up in the South, pale green rind has dark green stripes, red flesh, white seeds

How to prepare: European settlers, African Americans, and Native Americans all must have enjoyed most sorts of melons eaten raw by themselves or in fruit salads—but we have little documentation. We do know that watermelon rind pickles were preserved for winter use. (See recipe on page 67.)

OKRA
Abelmoschus esculentus (Hibiscus esculentus)

ORIGINALLY FROM NORTH Africa, okra was brought to America by slaves in the 1600s. A slippery texture is generally its most controversial characteristic, and it is just this quality that aficionados love and detractors find objectionable.

How to grow: Okra needs hot weather and full sun. Plant the seeds 6 inches apart in warm, organic-filled, well-drained soil and thin plants to 2 feet apart. Apply manure or fish meal after the pods have begun to set, and once again midway through the season. Okra requires about 1 inch of water a week. In cool-summer areas mulch plants with black plastic for extra warmth.

Japanese beetles, caterpillars, and stinkbugs are the few pests attracted to okra. Nematodes, verticillium wilt, and fusarium wilt are occasional problems.

Okra pods are best harvested when they are smaller than 3 inches long or they become woody and the plants stop producing. Use clippers to cut off the pod at its base.

Varieties

'Cow Horn': 65 days, 1865, vigorous plants, prolific producers, grows to 8 feet tall and the pods stay tender up to about 6 inches and grow to 1 foot long

'Green Velvet': late 1800s, velvety green pods, spineless, plants to 7 feet tall, pods excellent for pickling

'Red Okra': 65 days, red tender tasty pods ornamental plant to 5 feet tall has deep red stems, yellow-and-red flowers, and red pods

'White Velvet': 1890, tender large light green, pods, plant grows to 3 1/2 feet

How to prepare: If you find okra's slippery quality objectionable, add a little vinegar when cooking it. Okra has long been popular with people of many backgrounds in the South and is famous with seafood and in chicken soup and a stew commonly called gumbo, to which it adds flavor and thickening. The pods are also served boiled, fried, or pickled.

Below, from left: 'Red Okra' flower, 'Red Okra' pod, and 'Texas Longhorn' okra.

'Grampa Quierolo's' sweet red onion (*top*);
'Rocambole' garlic (*bottom*)

ONIONS
Bulbing Onions
Allium cepa

Potato Onions
(multiplier onions)
A. cepa var. *aggregatum*

*Rocambole (*serpent garlic, Italian garlic) *A. sativum* var. *ophioscorodon*

THE EGYPTIANS ENJOYED ONIONS five thousand years ago. Settlers brought all types of onions to this continent and especially valued the pungent varieties high in sulfur, because they could be stored well into winter.

How to grow: All members of the onion family prefer cool weather, particularly in their juvenile stage, and grow best in well-drained soil rich in organic matter and phosphorus. They are heavy feeders and should be fertilized, as well as evenly watered, throughout the growing season.

Bulbing Onions
Bulbing onions are generally grown from seeds. As biennials, onions bulb up the first year when grown from seed and flower the second.

It is important to select the right variety of onion for your climate and time of year because the bulbs are formed according to day length. Short-day onions bulb when they get 10 to 12 hours of light per day. They are most successful when spring planted in southern latitudes. Long-day onions require about 16 hours of sunlight each day to bulb up, which makes them ideal for northern areas.

Medium-day onions require 12 to 14 hours of light a day and do well in most parts of the country.

Start seeds inside in late winter or sow them $1/4$ inch deep outside in spring (or fall in mild climates). Although many gardeners plant them in rows or wide beds, onions can be interplanted among other vegetables. Fertilize with a balanced organic fertilizer when plants are about 6 inches tall and begin to bulb. Depending upon the variety, onions should be thinned to give each plant adequate room for unhampered development. Use the thinnings as scallions.

The most common pests attacking onions are the fly larvae known as the onion maggot and thrips. Thrips are attracted to stressed onion plants, especially those that are moisture stressed. See Appendix B (page 96) for more information.

Onions may be harvested anytime from the scallion stage to when they form mature bulbs. Storage onions are harvested after their tops die down, a process you can hasten by bending over the tops. To harvest them, dig up the onions and let them stay on top of the soil to dry out for at least a day. The bulbs must be protected from sunburn (which you can do easily by covering them with their tops). Place the bulbs on a screen or hang them where there is good air circulation to allow the skins to dry for several weeks before their final storage.

Varieties
Onions are much hotter in one part of the country than in another or when

grown in different soil. Lockhart Seeds carries a large selection of onions.

'Southport Red Globe': 110 days, 1873, long-day, large red onion with pungent flavor, good for northern gardens, good keeper

'Southport White Globe' ('White Globe'): 110 days, 1906, long-day, medium-size onion with white skin and flesh with a pungent flavor, can be used for a bunching onion, very adaptable

'Wethersfield' 'Red Large': 105 days, circa 1800, long-day, medium to large, sweet rose-white flesh, purple-red skin

'Yellow Ebenezer': 105 days, 1906, light yellow skin, off-white flesh, mild sweet flavor, good keeper

Potato Onions

These perennials divide to produce clusters of new 2- to 4-inch bulbs, hence the name potato onion. Plant a large potato onion bulb in early fall or early spring, and after the top dies down, a cluster of small bulbs will be found at its base. Harvest them and thoroughly cure. Break the clusters apart; eat some of the bulbs and reserve the rest for next year's crop. The small bulbs produce single medium onions, and the large ones produce clusters. If you plant a variety of bulb sizes, you will have both sizes for eating and at the same time keep a variety of sizes coming along all the time. Planting potato onions is a marvelous way to have onions in the garden most of the year without continually replanting.

'Yellow Potato Onion'

Varieties

'Yellow Potato Onion' ('Yellow Multiplier,' 'Mother Onion,' 'Pregnant'): pre-1790, 3-inch flavorful bulbs, quite drought tolerant and pink root resistant, good keeper, good for most areas except the Deep South

Rocambole

A rich-flavored, top-setting type of garlic with large, easily peeled cloves—also known as Italian garlic, hard-neck garlic, or serpent garlic—rocambole forms bulbils at the top of the stem. Either these bulbils or the cloves formed underground may be used in any recipe calling for garlic, or they can be planted to continue the crop.

Varieties

'German Red': very old, brought to America by German settlers in the 1700s, midseason, large, purple heads, yellow flesh, 8 to 12 cloves per head, large topsets

'Spanish Roja' ("Greek garlic"): late 1800s, midseason, hardneck type, 6 to 12 cloves per head, a Northwest heirloom, not for mildest-winter areas

How to prepare: Use the strong, "hot" onions and bulbing onions for a rich flavor in dishes that call for long cooking or caramelizing, such as onion soup or stews. The settlers creamed onions (see page 84) or used them to season vegetable soups, potato dishes, chowders, and vegetable puddings like corn pudding (see page 82). According to William Woys Weaver, the Pennsylvania Dutch used the leaves of the sprouts of 'German Red' rocambole in cabbage salads.

'Purple Top White Globe' turnips (*left*);
'Hollow Crown' parsnips (*above*)

PARSNIPS, RUTABAGAS, AND TURNIPS

Parsnips
Pastinaca sativa

Rutabagas
Brassica napus var. *napobrassica*

Turnips
B. rapa var. *rapifera*

ORIGINALLY FROM ASIA AND Europe, these wonderful, hearty vegetables represent security to many who live off the land, as they are easily grown and store reliably through the winter.

How to grow: These vegetables prefer cool weather and need well-drained, loose soil (free of rocks and obstacles) that will not impede their growth or contort their shape. Plant seeds ¼ inch deep in rows or wide beds. They will not transplant. If planted in good soil, they need little fertilizing but grow best with even, deep watering. Underwatered turnips and rutabagas taste bitter.

Timing is important when sowing parsnip seeds. Parsnips take from 100 to 130 days to mature. Since their starches are converted to sugars at cold temperatures (approaching 32°F), try to time the planting so roots may be touched by frost but harvested before the ground freezes. In mild-winter areas seeds can be sown in the late summer for a late-winter harvest. Parsnips can take up to three weeks to germinate. Thin the seedlings to 5 inches.

Turnips mature in 2 months, rutabagas in about 3 months. Plant rutabagas in early fall since frost improves their flavor. Thin rutabagas and turnips to 4 inches apart.

Parsnips are nearly free of pests and diseases. Turnips and rutabagas are sometimes attacked by flea beetles, cabbage root maggots, and cabbage caterpillars.

Parsnips may be left in the ground until early spring; cover them with a mulch in cold-winter areas. Turnip greens can be harvested when the plants are still young. Pick a few leaves from each plant and harvest until the greens get tough or bitter. The particular variety determines the harvest time for turnip and rutabaga roots. Generally speaking, harvest them when they are about the size of a tennis ball. Rutabagas remain of high quality when left in the ground.

Varieties

Parsnips
'Hollow Crown': 105 days, 12-inch tapered root, relatively free of side roots, fine-grained flesh, sweet flavor

'The Student': early; 1860; thick tapering roots 15 to 30 inches long, sweet mild flavor

Rutabagas
'America Purple Top': 90 days, pale yellow flesh with purple shoulders, sweet and fine grained, stores well

'Laurentian': 95 days, pre-1920s, from Canada, good keeper with uniform roots, turns orange when cooked

Turnips

'Gilfeather': 70 days, late 1800s, from Vermont, egg-shaped white roots with green shoulders, fine-textured sweet flesh

'Orange Jelly' ('Golden Ball'): 1854, yellow flesh (color varies with soil type), very sweet, exceptional turnip

'Purple Top White Globe': 55 days, pre-1880s, popular for both greens and roots, globes with white bottoms, purple shoulders, good keeper

How to prepare: Large old varieties of turnips were used like beets, as keepers for winter use. Turnips, rutabagas, and parsnips are great when boiled and combined with carrots or potatoes. They can be roasted in coals or the oven (see recipe, page 86) and served with meat, or added to stews and soups. Parsnips can be added like carrots to cakes. Says Debra Friedman, "Quite often, in Colonial times turnip roots were mashed. You don't find as many references to serving them whole or in chunks as you might find today. And quite often cooks of the time added cream and butter, or sometimes fat, to turnips, or even mixed turnips with mashed potatoes to make what they called turnip sauce."

PEAS
Shelling Peas
(garden peas, soup peas)
Pisum sativum

Edible-Podded Peas
(sugar snap peas, snow peas)
P. sativum var. *macrocarpon*

PEAS WERE KNOWN IN ANCIENT Egypt, Asia, and throughout central and southern Europe. Although peas were enjoyed when sweet and fresh in the spring, the settlers also dried them for use in winter soups and stews.

How to grow: Pea plants are either short bushes or long climbing vines. Peas require well-prepared, well-drained organic soil, full sun, high humidity, and cool weather. They tolerate some frost but do poorly in hot weather. Seeds should be planted 1 inch deep, 4 inches apart, in double rows 1 foot apart. Most varieties need some form of support, which should be placed in the ground at planting time. Peas need only a light fertilizing mid-season but profit from regular and deep watering—1 inch per week is ideal.

Seedlings are most attractive to slugs, snails, and birds, so it's best to cover them until they are 6 inches high. Control pea weevils by lightly dusting wet or dew-covered foliage with lime. See Appendix B (page 96) for information on moths, thrips, and mildew.

Ideally, peas should be harvested every day during the mature-pod stage. If left past maturity, they begin to lose their sweetness, and production

'Tall Telephone' (*above*); 'Yellow Podded' (*below*)

45

Purple flowers of 'Dwarf Grey Sugar' peas (*above*); 'Purple Podded' soup peas (*below*)

declines. Shelling peas are ripe when the pods are filled out but before they begin to lose their glossy green color. Let soup pea pods dry completely on the vine.

Standard Shelling Peas

'Alaska': 60 days, bush, 1880, named for a steamship that held a transatlantic speed record, wilt resistant, good fresh or dried

'Lincoln' ('Homesteader'): 70 days, bush, pre-1908, great tasting, not especially disease resistant

'Tall Telephone' ('Alderman'): 70 days, pole, named to honor Alexander Graham Bell, productive American pea that can grow to 8 feet, good flavor

Edible-Pod Peas

'Dwarf Gray Sugar': 75 days, bush, early, pre-1773, snow pea with 2-inch pods and lavender flowers, wilt resistant

'Risser Sickle Pea': pole, 1700s, English heirloom, very popular in Pennsylvania since Colonial times, 8 feet tall, sickle-shaped pods, good shelled or eaten whole

How to prepare: For generations, people have been enjoying fresh green peas just boiled and served with butter or added to a spring soup. In Colonial times, peas were mostly used dried and were used in winter soups that sometimes included ham and carrots.

PEPPERS
Capsicum spp.

CHILES HAVE BEEN USED IN DISHES in Mexico since about 7,500 B.C. and were highly regarded as a seasoning for every conceivable meat and vegetable. They were brought back to the Old World by Columbus, and their use quickly spread throughout southern Europe and into Asia.

How to grow: Peppers are a warm-weather crop. They cannot tolerate frost and won't set fruit unless the weather is between 65°F and 80°F. Start them indoors in flats 8 weeks before your average last frost date. When they are about 4 inches tall, any danger of frost is past, and the weather is warm, transplant them into the garden.

Plant the seedlings 2 feet apart, in full sun (or partial shade in hot climates). They require deep, rich soil and regular watering and fertilizing. Peppers are heavy feeders and respond well to regular applications of manure, fish emulsion, and kelp.

Young pepper plants can fall victim to snails, slugs, aphids, and cutworms. Otherwise, they are relatively pest free but are occasionally prone to the same diseases that afflict tomatoes.

Sweet peppers come in a wide range of colors. Once sweet peppers get near full size, pick them at their green, red, or yellow stage. Hot peppers can also be picked anytime, but most are hotter if allowed to ripen fully.

46

'Long Red Cayenne' (*top left*), 'Poinsettia' (*bottom left*), and 'Tabasco' peppers (*right*)

Varieties

Sweet Peppers

'Bull Nose' ('Sweet Bullnose,' 'Large Sweet Spanish,' 'Large Bell'): 60 days, green turning to red, 1759, from India, sweet flesh and slightly pungent ribs

'Cherry Sweet' ('Sweet Cherry,' 'Red Cherry'): 70 days, before 1860, red sweet, cherry-shaped peppers, great for pickling and stuffing

'Hungarian Paprika': 75 days, old variety good for drying and grinding, excellent flavor

Hot Peppers

'Long Red Cayenne' ('Long Cayenne'): 75 days, before 1827, slim peppers 5 inches long, very hot, grown for drying and grinding

'Poinsettia': 90 days, 2-foot plants bearing 2-inch upright pointed fruit, change from green to purple to red

How to prepare: Native Americans in the Southeast and West introduced peppers to the settlers. In New England some peppers were pickled and the cayenne types were dried and ground into a spice. Peppers were more common in the Southeast, especially where African slave women were the cooks. Peppers were added to gumbos, red beans, sausage, and jambalaya and were used as a seasoning in pickles, soups, and cooked vegetables. Bell peppers were used in chutneys and were stuffed. In the Southwest chiles were added to chili con carne and were used to season jerky, stews, and salsas.

POTATOES
Solanum tuberosum

POTATOES ORIGINATED IN THE
High Andes. They are full of vitamins,
minerals, some protein, and they are
filled with slow-burning fuel and fiber.

How to grow: Potatoes prefer cool
weather, and you can plant them in the
spring as soon as the soil has warmed
up. Potatoes are generally started by
planting pieces of the tuber that contain at least one "eye." Set them out as
soon as the ground can be worked in
the spring; if hard frosts are expected,
protect the young plants with floating
row covers. They are best grown in
well-drained, fertile, organic soil. For
an easy and large harvest, plant potatoes in trenches 6 inches wide by 6
inches deep, spaced about 1 foot apart
and covered with 4 inches of soil. As
the potatoes begin to sprout, fill in the
trench with more soil until it is level
with the existing bed or higher. For
highest production, keep the plants
moist. If planted with plenty of finished compost, potatoes generally
require little fertilizer.

Colorado potato beetles, flea beetles,
and aphids can attack potato foliage;
wireworms and white grubs can damage the tubers. The tuber pests are best
controlled by regular crop rotation. If
the soil is highly alkaline, potatoes
may develop a disease called scab;
change the pH of the soil to 6 if possible. If a plant shows signs of wilt,
blight, or viral disease, remove it and
throw it out.

When the foliage has died back, dig

tubers from one plant to check the crop
for tuber size. Dig carefully and at some
distance from the crown of the plant to
avoid damaging underlying tubers.
Although potatoes are generally harvested when their tops have died back,
you can prolong the season by harvest-

ing smaller tubers (called new potatoes)
once the plants start blooming.

Varieties

Ronniger's Seed and Potato Company
and Becker's Seed Potatoes are mail-
order sources specializing in potatoes.

'All Blue,' 'Green Mountain,' 'Blue Mechanic,' 'Menoninee,' 'All Red,' and 'German Finger' potatoes harvested at Seeds Blüm in Idaho

'**German Finger**': red-tan skin, yellow flesh, 1-5-inch-long tubers, excellent flavor, for boiling and salads

'**Green Mountain**': 90 days, 1885, from Vermont, large white potato with a light tan skin, very productive and adaptable

'**Peanut**'('**Giant Peanut**'): peanut-shaped fingerling, creamy yellow flesh, waxy texture excellent for salads, keeps well

Caution: Potato foliage, sprouts, and green tubers contain toxins that make them poisonous. Dispose of all portions of a tuber showing any green coloration.

How to prepare: Potatoes were a staple for the early settlers, who boiled, baked, roasted, and fried them. Potatoes were added to soups and stews, often along with other root vegetables. Cooks also mashed them and served them alone or mixed with other cooked root vegetables.

'**All Blue**': more than 80 days, purple blue flesh all the way through, medium-sized potatoes good for mashing, steaming, or baking

'**Bintje**': more than 90 days, 1911, Dutch, waxy yellow-skinned yellow-fleshed baking potato, out-standing flavor, high yield of large to medium-large tubers, quite disease free

'**Garnet Chile**': 90 days, 1853, red potatoes with white flesh, excellent for boiling, great keeper, the parent of most modern red potatoes

Harvest at Seeds Blüm includes 'White Icicle' and 'French Breakfast' (*top*), 'Early Scarlet Globe,' and 'Navet' radishes (*top and below*).

RADISHES
Raphanus sativus

RADISHES WERE EATEN IN ANCIENT Egypt, Greece, and Rome and have been cultivated in China and Japan for centuries. There are two types of radishes: the kind that grows and matures within 30 days, referred to as short-season or spring radishes, which are best when harvested young and do not store well, and what I call long-season radishes, the familiar daikon types popular in the Orient, long, fairly large ones that store well.

How to grow: Sow radish seeds directly in the garden after the last frost, or in early fall. Plant seeds $1/2$ inch deep and thin to 2 inches apart (even more for large-rooted varieties). Radishes can be planted in rows or wide beds. The soil should be light and well drained with a generous amount of compost. Radishes are light feeders, however, so they need little fertilizer. It is critically important to keep young radishes constantly moist to avoid cracking and a too-hot taste.

In some areas of the country, radishes are bothered by root maggots that are best controlled by rotating crops. Flea beetles can also be a considerable problem.

Generally speaking, short-season round radishes should be harvested when they are about the size of cherries—$3/4$ inch in diameter—or 1 inch across for the long, narrow type. If they are left in the ground too long, radishes have a tendency to get hot and

fibrous. Exceptions are some of the large, long-season radishes.

Varieties
Short-Season Radishes

'Early Scarlet Globe': 23 days, 1-inch globe-shaped roots with a mild sweet flavor

'French Breakfast' ('Early French Breakfast'): 23 days, 1879, red-and-white skin, mild, 1-inch diameter, long and narrow

'White Icicle' ('Lady Finger'): 27 days, 1896, crisp white flesh, old-time variety, grows up to 5 inches but is best if harvested sooner, more heat and drought tolerant than others

Long-Season Radishes

'Black Spanish': 75 days, very old, of medieval origin, deep purple, almost black skin with pure white flesh, stores up to 5 months

'Munchen Bier': 70 days, an old German radish with a tapered white root, traditionally sliced thin and served with salt and beer

How to prepare: Since radishes were an early and abundant spring crop, they were eaten raw a few times a day. They would be soaked in salt water and sliced. The young, tender radish greens were used too, either cooked or raw. When the plants flowered and produced seed pods, these were added to salads or pickled for winter use.

RHUBARB
Rheum rhabarbarum

RHUBARB WAS FIRST USED AS A medicinal herb in China two thousand years ago and probably originated in Siberia and southwest Asia. It was not used as a food in the West until the mid-1800s.

Caution: Rhubarb leaves are poisonous.

How to grow: Rhubarb is a long-lived herbaceous perennial that can grow to 5 feet tall. Its large green and red-veined leaves are dramatic atop their rosy red stalks.

Start rhubarb from rooted crowns available from local nurseries or mail-order companies. Three plants are adequate for the average family. Rhubarb needs cold winters and is not productive in areas with very hot summers.

Place the plants about 2 feet apart and situate the growing point of the crowns just at the soil surface. Rhubarb grows best in acidic, well-drained loam that is rich in organic matter. Mulch annually with manure. Water the plant until it is established; after that, watering is necessary only in arid climates. If placed correctly and given a modest amount of attention, a plant can last twenty years.

Do not harvest rhubarb stalks the first year. After that, in the spring harvest them by gently pulling off the thickest, healthiest stalks. Do not take more than half the stalks of any one plant.

Varieties
'Victoria' ('Myatt's Victoria'): pre-1837, said to have a "winy" flavor,

one of the earliest varieties, developed in England where rhubarb first became popular as a food crop

How to prepare: In many parts of the country rhubarb is the first "fruit" of spring. The thick, fleshy leaf stalks are used in sauces, pies, cobblers, and compotes. Stewed rhubarb has long been a spring favorite in this country, often combined with strawberries in dessert recipes. Rhubarb can also be made into jam or wine.

'Chipman's Red' rhubarb (*above*); rhubarb growing in Santa Cruz, California (*below*)

'Early Yellow Crookneck' (*above*) and
'Green-Striped Cushaw' squash (*below*)

SQUASH
Cucurbita maxima

Summer Squash,
C. mixta,

Winter Squash,
C. moschata,

Pumpkins,
C. pepo

THE NAME *SQUASH* COMES FROM
the Algonquin word *askutasquash*. The
many squashes are all New World
species, cultivated since pre-Columbian
times. The terms *squash* and *pumpkin*
are often used interchangeably.

How to grow: All squash, whether
classified as summer or winter, are
warm-season annuals. In short-
summer areas seeds must be started
indoors. The plants are usually grown
in hills, with two or three plants to a
hill. Space hills 6 feet apart for summer squash, and up to 10 feet apart for
winter squash and pumpkins. If seeding directly, plant seeds somewhat
more thickly and later thin to the
above distances. All squash need full
sun, rich organic soil, and ample water
during the growing season. They also
benefit from regular applications of
fish emulsion. Do not let the plants
dry out.

Squash bugs, spotted and striped
cucumber beetles, and (east of the
Rockies) squash vine borers may cause
problems. Expect mildew by the end of
the season in almost all climates. See
"Cucumbers" (page 37) and Appendix
B (page 96) for more information.

Pick summer squash once the blossoms have just withered, or up to when
they are still tender. It is important to
keep any excess summer squash
picked; otherwise, the plant drastically
slows its production.

Unlike summer varieties, winter
squash and pumpkins are picked when
they are fully mature. When winter
squash is fully ripe, the rinds will be
hard and the exterior color highly satu-
rated. Leave about 2 inches of stem
attached, or the squash is likely to rot.
Traditionally winter squash were
grown to be stored and eaten in winter.
While most varieties hold their flavor,
and some even get sweeter with storage, those held at too warm a temperature deteriorate.

Varieties
Summer Squash
'**Early Yellow Crookneck**' ('**Yellow
Crookneck**'): 50 days, bush, circa
1700, light yellow fruit with sweet
mild-tasting white flesh, pick while
young

'**Ronde de Nice**': 55 days, bush, French
heirloom, tender light green skin,
fine flavor, creamy texture, its
round shape lends itself well to
stuffing

Winter Squash
'**Boston Marrow**' ('**Autumnal
Marrow**'): 100 days, vining, pre-
1831, associated with the Iroquois,
very popular in the mid-1800s,
beautiful fruits to 20 pounds with
bright red orange skin and moist,
yellow orange flesh

'**Delicata**': 100 days, short vines, 1894,
dark green with yellow vertical

stripes, sweet 8-inch fruits similar in flavor and texture to sweet potatoes, heavy yield, stores well

'Green-Striped Cushaw' ('Striped Crookneck'): 110 days, vining, pre-1893, 10- to 15-pound fruit, creamy white skins with green stripes, slightly sweet yellow flesh, resistant to squash vine borer

'Hubbard' ('Green Hubbard,' 'True Hubbard'): 115 days, 1840s or before, warty dark green squash with moderately sweet yellow flesh, good keeper, 'Golden Hubbard,' 1898, and 'Blue Hubbard,' 1909, are subvarieties

Pumpkin

'Connecticut Field': 110 days, vining, pre-1700, these large pumpkins have been the standard jack-o'-lantern variety since the 1700s but are not the best for eating

'Rouge Vif d'Etampes' ('Red Etampes,' 'Cinderella'): 115 day, vining, 1883 in United States, 1830s in France, large flat "Cinderella" pumpkin with red-orange deeply fluted rind, mild squash flavor, was used by chefs in Paris in the 1800s as the base for soup stocks

'Seminole': 95 days, vining, cultivated

in Florida by the Seminoles in the 1500s, bell-shaped buff-colored fruits with sweet orange flesh, 7 inches in diameter, resistant to squash vine borer, good for hot, humid, disease-prone areas

How to prepare: Most old varieties of summer squash are quite similar to today's and can be used in the same ways: fried, stuffed, and added to soups and chowders.

Heirloom winter squashes and what were called pumpkins are quite similar to modern ones and can be used similarly. Debra Friedman notes, "Winter squashes and pumpkins were put into pies and puddings, which, of course, were side dishes for meals—they had not yet become desserts. Not until the twentieth century were pies and puddings accepted as dessert items. So you would find a squash pie or squash pudding served in addition to other vegetables, other starches, and meats." Squash or pumpkins were either boiled or baked before mashing them for pies, which were sweetened with sugar or molasses and sometimes apples. In 1749 Swedish naturalist Peter Kalm reported in *Travels in North America*, that the Native

Harvest of squashes and gourds (*top, left*); 'Boston Marrow' at Old Sturbridge Village (*top, right*); 'Rouge Vif d'Etampes' pumpkin (*below*)

Americans boiled pumpkins whole or roasted them in the ashes; that the settlers sliced and roasted them before the fire and sprinkled the cooked pulp with sugar; and that they boiled pumpkins and mashed them and then added milk. He also noted that pumpkin pulp was added to pancake dough and puddings.

Many varieties of sweet potatoes from the Seed Savers garden

SWEET POTATOES
Ipomoea batatas

SWEET POTATO VINES ARE perennials related to the morning glory and are native to the Andes, where they've been cultivated since pre-Incan times.

How to grow: Sweet potatoes must have long, hot summers to produce a good crop. They are planted in the spring by slips, which are sprouts produced by the roots. You may order slips from mail-order companies or start your own slips by placing the roots in a hotbed (a wooden tray with heating coils in the bottom that is filled with sand) about eight weeks before the weather warms up. Cover the roots with damp sand and maintain a hotbed temperature of 80°F. Pull off, don't cut, the shoots; they and their roots pull off easily.

To plant, dig and loosen the soil well and form mounds 8 inches high, about 4 feet apart. The soil should be sandy loam, not clay. Mix in a generous amount of organic fertilizer high in potassium and phosphorus. Bury the bottoms of the slips 4 inches deep and 1 foot apart. Keep the vines fairly moist until they are well established. When the transplants are about a month old, side dress with a balanced organic fertilizer.

A number of pests and diseases affect sweet potatoes. Check with your local university agricultural extension service, since problems differ by region.

Harvest sweet potatoes in late fall. Exposure to temperatures below 50°F causes the flavor and texture of roots to deteriorate. Sweet potatoes bruise easily, so dig and sort the roots carefully. Blemished or damaged roots should be used quickly, but undamaged sweet potatoes can be stored for up to six months.

Varieties

Because of local agricultural restrictions, sweet potato slips cannot be shipped into California. Fred's Plant Farm carries many varieties of sweet potatoes.

'Hayman': late 1800s, from the Eastern Shore of Maryland; white skinned; white flesh; highly aromatic

'Nancy Hall': 110 days; dry type; old variety with yellow skin and sweet, dark yellow flesh; resistant to soft rot; good keeper

'Southern Queen' ('White Yam,' 'Poplar Root'): 115 days, 1870, white skin and white flesh

How to prepare: In the South sweet potatoes were often used in dishes that would be made with squash or pumpkins in the North. That is, they were boiled, fried, baked, or used in puddings and casseroles. Later, in the 1800s, they were used to make pies. A Southern favorite, "candied sweets," is a method of cooking boiled sweet potatoes in a sauce of brown sugar and butter (see recipe, page 85). Sweet potatoes grew poorly in the North; when they were available, they were generally boiled and eaten with butter.

TOMATOES
*Lycopersicon lycopersicon
(L. esculentum)*

Currant Tomatoes
L. pimpinellifolium

TOMATOES WERE DOMESTICATED more than two thousand years ago in Mexico and Central America. Although not the most common vegetable with the settlers two hundred years ago, tomatoes are certainly one of the most popular heirlooms today.

How to grow: Tomatoes are heat-loving plants and can tolerate no frost. Extreme heat can sunburn the fruit, though, so it is necessary to protect them in extremely hot climates. Many varieties, especially the big slicing, heirloom, beefsteak types, do not set fruit well in temperatures in the high 90s (or under 50°F, either). Start plants from seed about six weeks before your last average frost date, planting them $1/4$ inch deep in good potting soil. Keep the plants in a very sunny window or under grow lights. When any danger of frost is over and the plants are about 6 inches high, transplant them into the garden, about 4 feet apart, in full sun and in well-drained soil amended with a good amount of organic matter. Plant the transplants deep—the soil should come up to the first set of new leaves. Stake or trellis the plants to save space and keep the fruit from spoiling on the ground. At transplant time and again when the fruit begins to set, fertilize tomatoes with fish meal, chicken manure, or a premixed organic fertilizer formulated for tomatoes. A form of calcium is often needed to prevent blossom-end rot. Liming may be needed every few years if you live in an area with acidic soil, as tomatoes prefer a soil pH about 6.5. Deep, fairly infrequent waterings are best. Mulch with compost after the soil has warmed thoroughly. A few major pests afflict tomatoes, including tomato hornworms, cutworms, tobacco budworms, nematodes, and whiteflies. A number of diseases are fairly common to tomatoes, including fusarium and verticillium wilt, alternaria, and tobacco mosaic.

Harvest tomatoes as they ripen. Color and a slight give to the fruit are the best guides to ripeness.

Varieties

Most heirloom tomatoes are quite climate-specific. Unfortunately, we have lost much growing information on the

'Brandywine' tomatoes

'White Beauty' tomatoes

'Old German Pink' ('Big Rainbow') tomatoes

'Brandywine' tomatoes

old-timers. When possible, look for varieties that grow well in your area.

Medium to Large Tomatoes

'Bonny Best': 76 days, old variety well loved for its tasty fruit, early producer, well adapted to northern gardens

'Brandywine': 80 days, 1889, Pennsylvania, large pinkish red tomato, loved by many, in the ideal climate this is the "gold standard" of tomato flavor and texture, grows poorly and produces insipid fruit in cool-summer areas and won't set fruit where summer nighttime temperatures are low or daytime temperatures are very high

'Cherokee Purple': 72 days, short vines, before 1890, from Tennessee, reportedly of Cherokee origin, unusual-colored purplish pinkish brownish tomato, full of flavor

'Earliana': 68 days, 1900, orange-red fruits with outstanding flavor, 'June

Pink' is a pink version of 'Earliana,' which produces longer

'Large Red': 85 days, prior to the Civil War one of the most commonly grown tomatoes in the United States, the fruits are deep red, heavily lobed, and rather flat in shape, flavor is sweet with a bit of tang

'Oxheart': 80 days, about 1925, large heart-shaped pink fruits, up to 2 pounds

'White Beauty' ('Snowball'): 80 to 85 days, creamy white, very sweet meaty fruit

Cherry Tomatoes

'Red Cherry' ('Old-Fashioned Red Cherry'): 72 days, pre-1840, full-flavored fruit, dependable vigorous plants resistant to fruitworm and heat

'Riesentraube': 70 days, probably grown by the Pennsylvania Dutch as early as 1855, recently reintro-

duced from a seed bank in East Germany, highly productive plants that produce large bunches of 1¹/₂-inch red pear-shaped fruit with excellent flavor

'Yellow Pear': 78 days, before 1805 (possibly dating to 1600s or earlier), bite-size yellow tomatoes shaped like small pears, low in acid, vigorous vines need staking, disease resistant

Currant Tomatoes

Huge plants that sprawl and reseed, the tiny currant tomatoes were grown and used by the early Americans.

'Red Currant': red version of the wild currant tomato, intensively flavored, thick skinned

'Yellow Currant': 62 days; indeterminate; related to the wild yellow currant tomato of South America; vines produce hundreds of ¹/₂-inch sweet, tart fruit; thick skinned, disease resistant, hardy

Processing Tomatoes

'**San Marzano**': 75 days, Italian heirloom, indeterminate, oblong great-
tasting paste tomato, good for canning or drying, vigorous plants

Seed Saving

Pick some of your best fruit just a day
or two past fully ripe. Place mashed
tomato pulp and seeds together in a
glass jar with $1/3$ cup of water. Allow
the mixture to ferment at room temperature for four days, or until obviously moldy. Stir the mixture on the
first and third days and skim off the
floating pulp and seeds on the second
and fourth days and discard. Retain
the seeds that have sunk to the bottom
of the brew. Rinse them with water,
spread them on paper towels, and let
them dry for a week. Place them in
air-tight containers for winter storage.

How to prepare: Yankees and
Southerners favored stewed tomatoes
with a little butter, sugar, and seasonings. Tomatoes were also made into
catsup, sun-dried to make what were
called tomato raisins, stuffed, or served
sliced with a dressing. Tomato "figs"
were made by scalding the tomatoes
and boiling them in one third their
weight in sugar. They were then flattened, sprinkled with sugar, and dried
in the sun to be stored for winter use.
They were also stewed with lima beans
and fat pork. According to William
Woys Weaver, in early American
kitchens, currant tomatoes were pickled both green and ripe and used like
capers to garnish fancy dishes.

'White Beauty,' 'Large Red,' 'Persimmon' yellow, 'San Marzano' paste, and 'Red Cherry'
tomatoes

cooking from the
heirloom
garden

You can cook most heirloom varieties the same way you do modern varieties. But there are exceptions worth noting—for example, some old varieties of snap beans need stringing, and most heirloom pea varieties were intended for drying and soup making, not for eating fresh. But only heirloom vegetables can be used in some unusual dishes—for instance, the large keeper beets and carrots are meaty enough for roasting or baking in the coals of a fire, but the small modern ones will shrivel up. See An Encyclopedia of Heirloom Vegetables (page 21) for details on cooking the most common heirloom vegetables.

Before the Europeans arrived, Native Americans cooked over open fires in containers made primarily of

The food historians at Old Sturbridge Village (*left*) give cooking demonstrations on site to show how foods were prepared in Colonial America.

pottery. Although they gathered much of their food from the wild, most tribes also maintained gardens of corn, beans, and squash—often referred to as the Three Sisters. They ground corn for porridge and cakes, which were cooked over coals; made succotash from both fresh and dried corn and beans; and roasted corn ears and squashes in the embers.

Corn was the Native Americans'

staple crop. To make the corn more digestible, they sometimes parched the kernels in the ashes before grinding them. In another process, they made hominy by treating the corn with lye, lime, or ashes to remove the skin (thus making the corn more digestible) and to render the nutrients more available. The hominied corn was used in stews and soups and was also ground to make the flat breads we know as tortillas. For more information on Native American foods, contact or visit Plimoth Plantation in Plymouth, Massachusetts, or write to Native Seed SEARCH in Tucson, Arizona (see Resources, page 102).

Over the years Native Americans shared their seeds and growing and cooking methods with the European settlers. In fact, there's evidence that without the Three Sisters the early settlers may not have survived. Of course, the Europeans had much to trade and share as well. They brought with them wheat, yeast, domesticated animals, many types of European vegetables, and metal cooking utensils. In time, a new cuisine emerged that blended the two cultures.

The early European settlers—mostly from England and, later, Germany—also brought an attitude about eating that was decidedly not based on vegetables. As Sandra Oliver wrote in *Food History News*, "In earlier times most people prized food with status and much needed calories—grains and meat." She went on to say that while they enjoyed fresh vegetables like the early spring greens and sweet new peas, "bread was the staff of life, and meat the primary objective of effort." Debra Friedman at Old Sturbridge Village said that often vegetables were a way of filling out the meal and sometimes a way to stretch

the meat. She gave as an example a recipe for adding pork to a pound of beans to make it go further (see recipe, page 74).

Vegetables may not have been of primary importance to the settlers, but they certainly are to me today. Ever in search of heirloom vegetable recipes (called receipts in the Colonial days), over the years I have found very few. Many of the old cookbooks devote whole sections to meats, seafood, preserves, pickles, and pastries but not to vegetables. One reason is that there was little need for detailing such basics as boiling beans or potatoes because young girls would have learned these techniques at their mothers' side. (Today's cookbooks wouldn't give you a recipe for a peanut butter sandwich or other common dishes, either.) Further, in that era women's work was

much less documented than the work of men—and it was the women who grew and cooked the vegetables. What information we do have comes from diaries, accounts of travelers, and a handful of cookbooks. Two American cookbooks I have found most informative are Amelia Simmons's, *American Cookery,* first published in 1796; and Lydia Marie Child's *The American Frugal Housewife Dedicated to Those Who Are Not Ashamed of Economy,* published in 1832. Another helpful book, first written in England and then made into an American version, is Mrs. Glasse's *The Art of Cookery Made Plain and Easy*. (The Simmons and Glasse books have both been reprinted by Applewood Books.)

Indications are that a large proportion of vegetables were preserved or stored for out-of-season use (especially

in rural settings where families had less access to markets, and among the working classes). Without refrigeration or canning, vegetables had to be preserved in other ways. For instance, cucumbers and watermelon rind were pickled; cabbages were stored whole in a root cellar, pickled, or made into sauerkraut; root vegetables, winter squashes, and pumpkins were stored in a cool cellar; and herbs, corn, onions, peas, and beans were dried.

Cooking in the 1600s and 1700s was done primarily on the open hearth. Fireplaces were equipped with andirons and a swinging crane to hold containers over the fire, and foods were boiled and fried in large cast-iron pots. Large Dutch ovens with a cover were used for baking. A good cook knew how and when to stack hot coals around the containers to maintain the correct temperature, a skill she would have learned from her mother. Most vegetables were boiled, baked in the coals, or fried, to be served as a side dish to meat; cooked up in pies, chowders, soups, and stews; or served cooked or raw as a salad with oil, vinegar, and sugar. Evidence suggests that by today's standards, vegetables were probably overcooked, though Mrs. Glasse cautions her readers against overcooking vegetables and thereby causing them to lose their color, and other old cookbooks recommend cooking a vegetable until just fork-tender. Foods in early America were prepared with large amounts of salt pork, butter, and cream—fitting for the heavy manual labor performed by most people in those days, but inappropriate for today.

The recipes that follow are examples of how to best enjoy heirloom vegetables. The majority of dishes are Native American, English, or German and reflect the foods of early New England, with other nationalities represented, plus a few recipes from the early South. Some recipes are representative of how foods would have been prepared years ago, but in many cases I have modified the recipes by cutting cooking times, reducing the fat and salt content, and recommending modern cooking methods (as few of us know how to cook well over an open hearth). If you are interested in authentic open-hearth cooking methods, consult the *Old Sturbridge Village Cookbook*.

A visit to Old Sturbridge Village shows authentic gardens filled with heirloom vegetables. Here (*left*) the gardeners gather seeds for the next season's gardens. Another 'living museum' is the village at Plimoth Plantation in Plymouth, Massachusetts. The demonstration gardens are filled with the 'Three Sisters'—corn, beans, and squash—interplanted the way the Native American tribes grew them in the Northeast.

Debra Friedman

Months after my visit with Christie White, I revisited Old Sturbridge Village to talk with Debra Friedman, program assistant for historic foodways, about heirloom vegetables and about what early Americans ate. Debra pointed out ways in which modern gardeners and cooks could learn from the old ways of cooking from the garden. "You can't beat the flavor—certainly not from the grocery store," Debra said. "And modern cooks could also enjoy some of the old recipes that call for using vegetables in different ways. Mashing turnips and potatoes together is wonderful—and baking beets or roasting vegetables with meat is fabulous. Also, some of the old varieties hold up better in soups or stews. Today we get exotic and overlook some of these wonderful old vegetables. Sometime when you're really busy and want to fix vegetables quickly and with little preparation, try some of the old cooking methods, such as boiling a dinner or baking vegetables."

We can also learn from the way our ancestors arranged meals, particularly how they carried over dishes from one meal to the next. Coleslaw, stewed beans, and squash pudding made for a meal one day would all be spread out the next day, even if there weren't enough of any one thing to go around. "If you had cold carrots and beef for supper one afternoon, they would be fried for breakfast or used in pies or puddings the next morning," said Debra. "Vegetables weren't considered just side dishes or eaten only for dinner, either. Though the cooking style was often less labor intensive, the diversity of each meal was rich. This meant eating a variety of foods at one meal, rather than our present-day 'nuclear' meal of just a meat, a starch, and a vegetable."

Debra explained that in the 1830s the main meal of the day, referred to as dinner, was served anytime between noon and two, depending on the family. It often consisted of boiled meat—most often beef, pork, or mutton—and three or four different boiled vegetables. The vegetables were usually mounded around the meat and served on one big pewter platter, or "charger." This platter was often the centerpiece of the meal and was surrounded by other dishes: puddings, vegetable pies, breads, cheeses, and pickles. Tea, or supper, was served between five and six in the evening and often consisted of leftovers from the earlier meal or "on hand" baked goods.

Desserts were often fruit preserved in sugar, and different kinds of cakes, gelatins, and custards. Pies and puddings were considered side dishes to meals rather than desserts. In fact, pie for breakfast was very common, as was pudding for breakfast or tea. A bowl of Indian pudding, made with corn meal, might be the main course for the evening meal rather than a dessert.

Our ancestors did not cook vegetables in the fancy ways that we do today. Most often vegetables were boiled, usually until they were at least fork tender. Butter—lots of butter—or occasionally lard, cream, salt, pepper, or vinegar were used as seasonings. Vegetables were also commonly roasted in meat drippings in the pan or in the coals of a fire.

"Most vegetables were cooked in this era," Debra said. "Not many people ate them raw. We don't find recipes for raw vegetables, so we don't know if our ancestors ever just went out and ate a carrot or some celery from the garden. They would serve radishes raw, but not many other vegetables. In fact, a vegetable we always eat raw, cucumbers, was considered

Debra Friedman is the program assistant for historic foodways at Old Sturbridge Village in Sturbridge, Massachusetts.

inedible when raw, as it was not easily digested, so it was served fried or stewed. Vegetables served at breakfast were generally fried, a quick cooking method, and at dinner they would be boiled, baked, or roasted, all long-cooking methods. Furthermore, fresh annual vegetables were eaten for only a few weeks during the summer; vegetables were dried or stored for the rest of the year.

"You also don't find much primary source documentation about what herbs our ancestors cooked with, but that's not to say they didn't use any," Debra said. "A lot of recipes say 'season to taste,' or occasionally, 'add sweet herbs,' though they don't usually say what herbs or how much to add. We know they did incorporate herbs in some dishes, particularly in different kinds of beans. Recipes say

to boil beans with parsley or summer savory. But obviously not many herbs were used. I think it would depend on the cook. Instead, to add flavor to dishes, they served spices and condiments as side dishes, or made sauces of different kinds of herbs and put them on the meat or vegetables. For instance, they used horseradish sauce for beef, and sage in the stuffing. They used vinegars and cucumbers— they made cucumbers into a sauce for fish. Parsley, butter, and capers combined to make a sauce for chicken.

"In early America most vegetables were boiled, and the cooking water was generally discarded. In fact, recipes often said to use enough water to remove any bad taste and to drain the vegetables well.

"In fact, glorifying vegetables wasn't part of the traditional English diet they inherited. That diet consisted more of meat and starch than of vegetables. So, in the nineteenth century, you find the same old vegetables served over and over again, with few of the varieties we have today. Stressing fresh vegetables in the diet is a very, very new idea."

Talking with Debra certainly made me aware that, like central heating and running water, being able to eat a variety of vegetables fresh from the garden is a luxury of the twentieth century that I certainly wouldn't want to give up.

About Pickles

Our ancestors pickled many vegetables to preserve them for winter eating. Salt and acetic acid in the vinegar inhibited the growth of microorganisms that rotted food or even made it toxic. Cucumber was the most common vegetable that was pickled, but beets, green beans, cabbages, radish pods, okra, and hot peppers were also preserved. Watermelon rind pickles were especially popular in the Mid-Atlantic states.

In the 1700s, pickles were either "put down" in a large stoneware crock and covered with a towel or "put up" in a sealed jar that was covered by either leather or a pig's bladder secured with string. These coverings were applied wet and would shrink to seal the container as they dried. Unfortunately, spoiled pickles were a common occurrence. In the mid-1800s Louis Pasteur proved that bacteria that spoil food could be killed by heat, and soon cooks were canning their pickles.

If you follow modern pickling methods carefully, you can prevent molds, yeasts, and bacteria that spoil food or cause food poisoning (including the fatal toxin produced by the botulism bacteria, *Clostridium botulinum*) from growing in your pickles.

The following three recipes, if refrigerated, keep well for a few weeks. For long-term storage, the jars need to be processed in a canner using the water bath method. This method is suitable for canning pickles because of their high acid content. (Most unpickled vegetables must be canned in a pressure canner to make them safe.)

Pickling is not that difficult if you follow the steps below. Here are a few tips:

• Pickle only fresh vegetables.

• Don't use hard water as it can cause soft pickles.

• Use a canner—a twenty-one- or thirty-three-quart capacity kettle that comes with a jar rack and a lid. Canners are designed to hold enough water to cover the jars completely. The rack keeps the jars from touching the bottom of the pan and allows them to be surrounded by the water.

• Use pickling salt, not iodized salt as it darkens pickles.

• For safety, always use the exact proportions of ingredients indicated in the recipe.

• Choose vinegar with a 4 percent to 6 percent acetic acid (40 to 60 grain) content.

To Prepare Jars for Canning

1. Select commercial canning jars and check them for chipped sealing surfaces.

Canning Your Pickles

Make pickles according to the recipes that follow. Canning time and jar size is given for each recipe.

1. Pack the pickles in the still-hot jars and add enough liquid to fill the jar up to within 1/2 inch of the rim.

2. Run a rubber spatula gently around the pickles to release any air bubbles, then thoroughly clean the rim.

3. Place the sterilized lids on the jars, then tighten the bands over the lids.

4. Fill the canner with enough water to cover the jars with 2 inches of water. Bring the water to a boil.

5. Once the water is boiling in the canner, arrange the jars in the rack and using its handles lower it gently into the water. Cover the canner. Adjust the heat to maintain a simmer.

6. Set a timer for the amount of time recommended in the recipe, starting the timer as soon as the jars are in the canner. (Remember to add one minute to the given time for every thousand feet you are above sea level.)

7. If needed, add more boiling water to keep the water level at least an inch above the jars.

8. Once the recommended canning time has elapsed, remove the jars from the canner using a jar lifter and place them on a clean towel. Provide six inches of space between the jars for even cooling.

9. After twenty-four hours check the seals on the jars. A sealed lid will not "give" if you press on it hard with your thumb. Remove the bands. The lid should be tight enough that you can

lift the jar by the lid. If any lids are loose, refrigerate the jar and use its pickles right away.

10. Label the jars and store them in a cool, dark closet. For best quality use them within a year.

11. Before opening a jar that has been stored, check for a bulging lid, molds, leakage, cloudy liquid, bubbles, or other signs of spoilage. Under no circumstances should you taste any pickle that is slightly suspect. Dispose of any spoiled pickles in the garbage.

Dill Pickles, Fresh Packed

Note: Pickling spices are a combination of mustard seeds, allspice, bay leaves, black pepper, celery seeds, and cloves.

> 17 to 18 pounds pickling cucumbers
> Approximately 2 gallons 5 percent brine solution (1 1/2 cups salt dissolved in 2 gallons of water)
> 6 cups distilled or cider vinegar
> 3/4 cup pickling salt
> 1/4 cup granulated sugar
> 2 tablespoons pickling spices tied in a small cheesecloth sack
> 14 teaspoons mustard seeds (2 teaspoons per quart)
> 7 tablespoons dill seeds (1 tablespoon dill seeds per quart)
> Optional: 7 fresh dill flower heads

Wash the cucumbers well, scrub them to remove any dirt, and drain. Cover them with the brine and let them sit overnight.

The next day, drain the cucumbers. In a large saucepan, combine the vinegar, salt, and sugar with 9 cups of

2. Wash the jars in soapy water and rinse them well.

3. Place jars in a large pot, cover with hot water, and bring to a boil. Boil for 10 minutes. If you are canning at more than one thousand feet above sea level, add one more minute of boiling time for every additional thousand feet. Leave the jars in the hot water until you are ready to use them.

4. In a small saucepan, boil the metal bands (or "rings") and the lids for five minutes and leave them in the water until you are ready to use them.

water. Add the sack of pickling spices and bring to a boil. Lower the heat, but keep the liquid hot. Pack the cucumbers in 7 sterilized, hot, 1-quart canning jars. Divide the mustard seeds, dill seeds, and dill flower heads (if using), among the jars. Discard the pickling spices and cover the cucumbers in each jar with the boiling vinegar solution to within 1/2 inch the top of the jar. Tighten the jar bands.

Simmer the jars in a water bath for 20 minutes in a canner.

Remove the jars from the water and allow to cool.

Makes 7 quarts.

Radish Pods

Radish pods develop after the flowers die back and the seeds start to form. A recipe from The *Skilful Housewife's Book* (1846) reads: "Gather them in sprigs or bunches, young and tender and letting them stand in salt and water three days; then pickle like cucumbers."

Pickled Dilly Beans

2 pounds string beans: 'Blue Lake,' 'Kentucky Wonder,' or any other long, tender, green string bean
3 dill seed heads
1 cup white vinegar
2 tablespoons salt
1 teaspoon dill seeds
1 teaspoon mustard seeds
8 whole black peppercorns

Wash the beans thoroughly and trim the ends. In a large pot of boiling water blanch the beans for 2 minutes. Drain and then pack them lengthwise into three hot sterilized pint jars. Place a dill seed head along the inside of each jar so it is visible on the outside of the jar. Combine the vinegar with 3 cups of water, the salt, and the spices and bring it to a boil. Cover the beans with the boiling liquid, leaving 1/4 inch head space. Place lids on the jars and tighten bands. Process jars in a boiling water bath for 20 minutes. Let the jars cool and then store them in a cool, dry place.

Makes 3 pints.

Grandma Dorothy's Watermelon Pickles

My husband's grandmother taught me how to make these great pickles. I serve them with chicken curry and pork, and I tuck them in ham and tuna sandwiches. Sometimes I vary the recipe by adding a sliced lemon and a few inches of fresh ginger cut into pieces.

Approximately 1 medium watermelon
1 tablespoon salt
2 cups distilled or white wine vinegar
4 cups sugar
1 1/2 cinnamon sticks
20 whole cloves

Cut the watermelon into large sections. Taking one section at a time, peel the

green skin off the rind and trim off the pink portion. The 'Blackstone' variety has a particularly thick rind perfect for pickling. (You need 8 cups of cubed, trimmed rind.) Set the watermelon flesh aside to use for a salad. Cut the rind into 1-inch squares. In a large pot, cover the rind with water, add the salt, and bring to a boil over high heat. Simmer until the rind is tender, about 10 minutes. Pour the rind into a colander and rinse it in cold water. In a large bowl, cover the rind with ice water for at least 10 minutes. In a large pot, boil together the vinegar, sugar, cinnamon, and cloves. (Add the ginger and lemon at this point if desired.) Drain the ice water from the bowl of rind chunks and place the rind in the syrup, simmering until the rind becomes clear, about 10 minutes. Pack the boiling rind into hot sterilized pint or half-pint canning jars, filling them to within $1/2$ inch of the rim with syrup. Clean the rim, adjust the bands, and process, the filled jars in a canner water bath for 10 minutes.

Makes 2 to $2^{1}/_{2}$ pints.

Heirloom Tomato Platter

Homegrown heirloom beefsteak tomatoes, such as 'Brandywine' and 'Big Rainbow,' can be shown off to advantage on a platter and drizzled with this simple but tangy dressing.

6 to 8 large beefsteak tomatoes
(approximately 4 pounds)
Garnish: fresh basil or mint leaves

For the vinaigrette:

1 teaspoon Dijon mustard

2 tablespoons fresh lemon juice

1 tablespoon dry white wine

1 tablespoon fresh minced basil or mint

1/2 cup extra-virgin olive oil

Salt and freshly ground black pepper

To make the vinaigrette: In a bowl, whisk together the mustard, lemon juice, wine, and basil to combine. Slowly whisk in the oil, beating continually until the dressing is thoroughly blended. Add salt and pepper to taste. Refrigerate.

Just before serving, slice the tomatoes. On a large platter, lay them out in a decorative pattern. Drizzle the vinaigrette over the tomatoes. Garnish with fresh basil.

Serves 6 to 8.

Summer Squash and Corn Chowder

This soup uses copious amounts of summer squash and is substantial enough eat as a light supper. Serve it with corn bread and a green salad.

To remove kernels from the cob, cut a small piece off the blunt end to make it straight across, place the cob blunt-end down on a cutting board, and use a sharp knife to cut off the kernels. (Mail-order companies carry a gizmo for cutting the kernels off more easily.)

7 or 8 young 5- to 6-inch-long
  summer squash (about 2
  pounds)
2 tablespoons unsalted butter or
  vegetable oil
1 large onion, finely chopped
$1/2$ teaspoon dried thyme
2 cups fresh sweet corn kernels
  (about 5 ears of corn)
$2^{1}/_{2}$ cups milk
1 cup heavy cream
Salt and freshly ground black
  pepper to taste
$1/8$ to $1/4$ teaspoon ground red pepper
Garnish: sour cream

If you can pierce the skins easily with your fingernail, the squash do not need peeling; otherwise, peel them. Grate the squash; you should have about 8 cups. Steam the squash in a large steamer until tender, approximately 15 minutes. Mash the squash and put it aside.

In a large Dutch oven, melt the butter and over medium heat sauté the onion and thyme for about 5 minutes until translucent but not brown. Remove from heat and add the squash, corn, milk, and cream. Season with salt and peppers. Over medium heat stir the mixture to heat it thoroughly; do not bring the mixture to a boil, or it will curdle. Serve garnished with sour cream.

Serves 4 to 6.

Gourd Soup

Should be made of full-grown gourds [small squash] but not those that have hard skins; slice three or four and put them in a stewpan, with two or three onions, and a good bit of butter; set them over a slow fire till quite tender (be careful not to let them burn); then add two ounces of crust of bread and two quarts of good consommé, season with salt and cayenne pepper; boil ten minutes or a quarter of an hour; skim off all the fat. And pass it through a tamis (sieve); then make it quite hot, and serve up with fried bread.

—Mrs. N. K. M. Lee, 1832,
The Cook's Own Book

This recipe is Debra Friedman's updated version.

8 tablespoons salted butter, divided
4 pounds butternut or other winter
  squash (about 4 large squash),
  peeled and sliced thin
4 onions, sliced
1 loaf of white bread
2 quarts homemade chicken or beef
  broth, or 5 ($14^{1}/_{2}$-ounce cans)
  commercial broth
Salt
Ground red pepper

In a large Dutch oven, melt 4 tablespoons of the butter and over medium heat sauté the squash and onions until the squash is tender and the onions are translucent, about 15 minutes, stirring frequently to prevent burning. Turn off the heat. Meanwhile, toast three slices of bread and break them into crumbs.

Add the broth and bread crumbs to the squash mixture and season with salt and ground red pepper to taste. Return the Dutch oven to the heat and simmer 15 minutes until the squash is tender enough to pass through a colander. Meanwhile, cut the remaining bread into 1-inch cubes. In a large sauté pan, melt the remaining 4 tablespoons butter and sauté the bread cubes over medium heat for about 5 minutes until golden brown, stirring occasionally to prevent burning. Set them aside. Pour the soup through a colander, return it to the Dutch oven, and heat to serving temperature. Serve the soup in individual bowls and top with the bread cubes.

Serves 6 to 8.

Borscht

What comfort this hearty soup must have brought to Russian immigrants and other Central Europeans adjusting to the food in their new land. Rustic rye or pumpernickel bread with lots of butter accompanies this soup perfectly.

4 tablespoons vegetable oil, divided

1¹/₂ pounds lean beef cut into
    1-inch cubes, divided

2 medium onions, chopped

1 bay leaf

3 medium potatoes, cut into eighths

3 cups raw beets (6 to 8 medium
    beets), peeled and shredded

1 cup raw carrots (2 or 3 medium
    carrots), peeled and shredded

1/2 medium cabbage, shredded

1/4 teaspoon freshly ground black
    pepper

3 tablespoons tomato paste

1 garlic clove, pureed

4 tablespoons cider vinegar

1/4 teaspoon celery seeds

1/4 teaspoon salt

Garnish: light sour cream and fresh
    dill

In a large Dutch oven, heat half of the oil and over medium heat brown half the beef for about 10 minutes. Remove it from the heat and onto a plate. Repeat the process with the rest of the beef. Add the onions toward the end of the cooking and cook them until translucent. Remove from heat, add 2

quarts of water to the Dutch oven, then the reserved beef, and the bay leaf. Over low heat, simmer for about 1 hour, until the meat is tender. Remove the bay leaf and skim off any scum.

Add the potatoes, beets, carrots, cabbage, pepper, tomato paste, garlic, vinegar, salt, and celery seeds. Reduce heat to very low and simmer for another 30 to 45 minutes, or until the vegetables are tender. Do not bring the mixture to a boil, or the color will change from red to brown. Adjust the seasonings. The borscht is ready to serve at this point, but it will improve slightly if refrigerated and then reheated the next day. Garnish with sour cream and dill.

Serves 8.

Cold Slaw and Hot Slaw

Here are recipes for Cold Slaw and Hot Slaw from the past.

Select the hardest, firmest head of cabbage. Cut it in two, and shave it as fine as possible. A cabbage cutter is best. It must be done evenly and nicely. Lay it in a nice deep dish. Melt together vinegar, a small piece of butter, pepper, a little salt. Let it scald and pour over it.

—Mrs. L. G. Abell, *The Skilful Housewife's Book,* 1846

[Hot Slaw] is made in the same manner [as cold slaw], except it is laid in a sauce pan with the dressing, and just scalded, but not boiled. Send it to the table hot.

—Mrs. L. G. Abell, *The Skilful Housewife's Book,*1846

For a modern version of hot slaw, try the following:

    1 medium head cabbage, finely
        shredded
    1/4 cup butter
    1/4 cider vinegar
    1/2 teaspoon pepper

Put all the ingredients in a large frying pan or wok over medium heat. Cover and cook about 5 minutes, or until the cabbage starts to wilt, stirring frequently. Serve immediately.

Variation: Add 1 tablespoon finely snipped fresh dill or other garden herbs and 1/4 to 1/2 cup each of finely chopped or shredded carrots, green beans, and/or peas, 1 teaspoon mustard seeds, and 1 teaspoon sugar or 1/4 cup apple juice. Then cook as above.

Serves 6 to 8.

German Potato Salad

I first tasted this recipe when my mother-in-law, Margaret Creasy, made it, and it was my first introduction to German-style cooking. It is more Pennsylvania Dutch than old-country German, however. (The name is confusing; for years I thought the word *Dutch* in this context referred to the Netherlands, not to *deutsch,* meaning German.) Cooks in that part of Pennsylvania have been making it for years.

    8 medium potatoes (11/2 to 2
        pounds)
    3/4 cup vinegar (cider or white)
    3/4 cup sugar
    1/2 teaspoon salt
    1 rounded tablespoon flour, or 1/2
        tablespoon flour and 1/4 table-
        spoon cornstarch
    8 slices uncooked bacon, diced
    3/4 cup diced onion

Boil the potatoes until just tender, 20 to 30 minutes. Then drain, peel, and cut them into 1/4-inch slices. Put them into a serving bowl, and set aside.

Meanwhile, in a small saucepan, combine the vinegar, sugar, salt, and 1/2 cup of water and bring the mixture to a boil. In a small bowl, mix the flour with about 1/4 cup of water, stir it into the vinegar mixture, and simmer briskly, stirring occasionally, until translucent and thickened, about 10 minutes.

In a skillet, fry the bacon and onions until golden brown, then add them (including the bacon fat) to the vinegar mixture. Pour the mixture over the potatoes while they are still warm, and mix gently. Let the potato salad stand at room temperature for about 2 hours, stirring every half hour or so. Refrigerate if not using at once, but serve at room temperature or slightly warmed.

Serves 6 to 8.

Spring Vegetable Soup with Parsley Dumplings

This is a basic soup that can be varied from season to season and from garden to garden. Serve with a rustic bread and a salad on the side.

For the stock:

1 chicken, approximately 4 pounds
1 onion, unpeeled
4 celery ribs
2 large carrots
2 garlic cloves
1 bay leaf
2 teaspoons thyme
2 teaspoons salt

For the soup:

2 cups halved or quartered baby
  potatoes
1¹/₂ cups sliced carrots (about 4
  medium carrots)
1 cup sliced celery (about 2 ribs)
1¹/₂ cup shelled young peas (about
  1 pound unshelled)
1¹/₂ cups sliced asparagus (1-inch
  pieces) (about 1 pound
  asparagus)
1 cup sliced scallions (1 bunch)
2 cups young spinach leaves
2 cups young dandelion greens
Salt and freshly ground black
  pepper

For the dumplings:

1 egg
¹/₂ cup all-purpose flour
3 tablespoons parsley, minced
¹/₂ teaspoon salt
¹/₈ teaspoon freshly ground nutmeg

To make the stock: Remove the skin and fat from the chicken. Cut it into pieces and set aside the breasts. Put the legs, thighs, wings, back, and neck into a large stockpot. Add the onion, celery, carrots, garlic, bay leaf, and thyme. Add 5 quarts of cold water and the salt and bring to a boil. Cover the stockpot and simmer over low heat for 2 hours. Remove the chicken and vegetables from the pot. Discard the vegetables, reserve the chicken, and set aside the broth.

To make the soup: Bring the stock to a boil and add the reserved chicken breasts, the potatoes, carrots, celery, and peas. Simmer for 10 minutes, then add the asparagus and scallions and simmer for 5 more minutes. Remove from heat. Remove the chicken breasts and drain them.

To make the dumplings: In a small bowl, blend the egg, flour, parsley, salt, and nutmeg with a fork until smooth. Bring the soup to a rolling boil. Dip a soup spoon into the boiling liquid, then use it to scoop out a small amount of batter from the bowl. Drop the spoonful of batter into the soup. The batter will drop easily from the spoon if you first dip the spoon into the boiling liquid each time. The

dumplings rise to the surface when they are done. Cut the chicken breasts into cubes; remove the meat from the reserved thighs, wings, and back; and add them to the soup. Add the spinach leaves and dandelions greens and adjust seasoning with salt and pepper. Heat the soup to serving temperature and ladle it into warm bowls.

Serves 6.

Wild Greens with Bacon and Eggs

Early Americans welcomed the greens of spring, either from the garden or growing wild, such as dandelions and violets (*Viola Odorata*).

6 small eggs

8 cups lightly packed greens such
   as spinach, dandelions, mâche,
   or violet leaves

1/3 pound thick-sliced bacon, cut in
   1-inch pieces

1 small onion, minced

1/4 cup brown sugar

1/2 teaspoon dry mustard

1/2 teaspoon cornstarch

1/4 cup cider vinegar

Freshly ground black pepper

Place the eggs in a saucepan of cold water, bring to a boil, and immediately remove from heat. Let the eggs sit for 15 minutes, drain the water from the saucepan, then run cold water over the eggs. Let them cool, and then peel them and set them aside.

Wash the greens well and dry them in a salad spinner. Break leaves into bite-size pieces and refrigerate.

In a large pan, sauté the bacon until crisp. Drain the bacon on a paper towel. Remove all but 1/4 cup of bacon drippings from the pan. Over medium heat sauté the onion until transparent,

about 5 minutes.

In a small bowl, blend together the sugar, mustard, and cornstarch. Add the vinegar and 2/3 cup water and whisk together. Add the mixture to the onion and blend, cooking over low heat for 1 minute, until it starts to thicken.

Cut the eggs in half. On four salad plates equally divide the greens to form a bed. Drizzle a quarter of the still-warm dressing on each plate. Garnish with the bacon pieces and 3 egg halves. Grind pepper on top and serve.

Serves 4.

Mess o' Greens

Greens have long been a tasty and nutritious staple in the rural South. Most gardeners know that they are one of the easiest crops to grow in abundance. In fact, for generations housewives and children would gather greens from the wild, namely chicories, mustards, and in the South, the tender shoots of pokeweed. Picking pokeweed took special knowledge as the plants are toxic at certain times of the year.

This variation on a traditional preparation method opts for a minimum of water and cooking time, to retain nutrients and flavor. Note that the parenthetical equivalent measure in cups is for 2 pounds of each kind of green. When preparing greens, remove all tough stems unless you are using young chard—its stems are tender and tasty. Some parboiled, diced potatoes added to the greens are good too.

1/4 to 1/2 pound bacon or salt pork, coarsely chopped

2 pounds or so of greens: mustard (12 cups), collards (14 to 16 cups), kale (16 cups), dandelions (12 to 16 cups), or chard (16 cups), washed and torn or chopped

1/4 cup cider or red wine vinegar

1/8 to 1/4 cup sugar

1 teaspoon dry mustard

Freshly ground black pepper

In a large skillet, fry the bacon until crisp. Add the greens, vinegar, sugar, dry mustard, pepper, and 1/2 cup of water. Cover and cook over medium heat for 3 to 5 more minutes, or until the greens are tender. The cooking time will vary depending on the greens you use. Uncover pan and cook off excess liquid, or serve it Louisiana-style as "pot likker," in a separate bowl as an accompaniment.

Serves 6 to 8.

Beans with Pork

In early America baked beans were not a vegetable dish but a pork dish; the beans were used to stretch the meat portion of the meal. The bean dish with molasses and salt pork we know today was first reported in 1840. This recipe is based on one from *The American Frugal Housewife,* by Lydia Marie Child.

1 pound 'Soldier,' 'Jacob's Cattle,' or 'Great Northern' beans

1 tablespoon vegetable oil, or 1/4 pound salt pork, cut into 1-inch cubes

1 pound lean pork, fresh pork shoulder, or boneless pork chops, cut into 1-inch-wide strips

1 medium onion, chopped

1/3 teaspoon dried thyme

Freshly ground black pepper

1/4 teaspoon salt

Pick over the beans, removing any debris, and wash them. Place them in a large saucepan and cover them with 2 inches of water. Either let them sit overnight or bring them to a boil for 1 minute, then remove from the heat and let them sit for 1 hour.

Cook the beans for 1 to 1 1/2 hours until they are just tender. Drain them, setting the bean liquid aside.

In a large skillet heat the oil (if using salt pork, sauté it for 2 or 3 minutes) and over fairly high heat brown half of the pork on all sides. Transfer it to a bean pot or a 3-quart covered Dutch oven. Repeat the process with the rest of the pork. Pour off the remaining grease. Carefully deglaze the pan with a little of the bean water and pour it over the pork. Add the beans, onion, thyme, pepper, and salt (omit the salt if you are using salt pork). Mix the ingredients and add enough bean liquid to just cover the beans. If you don't have enough liquid, add a little stock or boiling water. Cover the bean pot.

Bake at 300°F for 4 to 6 hours. Check occasionally to make sure the liquid still covers the beans. If it gets too low, add more bean liquid or boiling water. Half an hour before the beans are done, uncover and let the beans brown slightly on top.

Serves 6 to 8.

Corn Bread

Corn bread has infinite variations, which is one reason for its popularity as a staple food. It may be cooked on a griddle, in a skillet, or in the oven. The cornmeal may be yellow, blue, white, or red; be ground coarse or fine; or include wheat flour for a lighter bread. Sometimes the bread is sweetened; other times it is seasoned with minced vegetables, herbs, peppers, or cheese. One constant is the delicious flavor of corn bread—especially when it's made with homegrown cornmeal. This recipe is a modern version with some suggested additions. For its wonderful novelty, I sometimes use blue cornmeal made from 'Hopi Blue' corn and add some minced red peppers.

1 1/2 cups corn meal

1/2 cup whole-wheat pastry flour or
    unbleached white flour

1 1/2 teaspoons baking powder

1/2 teaspoon salt

1 egg

1/4 cup vegetable oil

1/8 to 1/4 cup brown sugar, honey,
    or maple syrup

1 cup whole milk

Up to 1 cup of minced, briefly
    sautéed vegetables such as
    sweet and/or hot peppers and
    onion (optional)

About 1/4 cup minced herbs, such
    as basil, parsley, or cilantro
    (optional)

1 teaspoon cumin or chili powder,
    or 1/4 cup grated sharp cheese
    (optional)

Heat the oven to 400°F.

Sift together the cornmeal, flour, baking powder, and salt. In a bowl, beat the egg and add the oil, sugar, and milk. Stir in the dry mixture (and any of the optional ingredients) and mix briefly. Pour the mixture into a greased standard loaf pan, 8-inch-square baking pan, or muffin tin, and bake for about 30 minutes (20 minutes for muffins), or until golden brown.

Makes 1 loaf.

New England Boiled Dinner

A boiled dinner was a favorite cold-winter-night dish. It could have been boiled up over the fire a good part of the day, needing little attention. Further, leftovers could be cooked up in hash the next day. Avoid the plastic-wrapped brisket from the supermarket, as it is tough and fatty. Get a lean one from a butcher. Serve with mustard, horseradish, and/or pickles.

3 to 4 pounds extra-lean corned beef brisket

2 tablespoons pickling spice in cheesecloth bag, or 6 whole cloves, 4 whole allspice, $1/2$ teaspoon peppercorns, 1 tablespoon mustard seeds, and 2 bay leaves in cheesecloth bag

5 or 6 medium potatoes, quartered

5 or 6 medium carrots, cut into chunks

2 large onions, thickly sliced

4 turnips and/or 4 golden beets, peeled and quartered (optional)

1 medium head cabbage, cut into 6 or 8 wedges

For the glaze:

$1/3$ cup Dijon mustard

$1/4$ teaspoon ginger or cloves

2 tablespoons brown sugar

In a large kettle or Dutch oven, cover the meat with water. Boil for half an hour; pour off the water and discard it. Add fresh boiling water to cover the meat, add spices, and simmer for 45 minutes per pound of meat (minus the first half hour), or until fork-tender. Remove the meat to an ovenproof pan, fat-side up. Add the potatoes, carrots, and onions (and turnips and beets, if desired) to the kettle, cover, and boil for 15 minutes. Place the cabbage on top of the other vegetables and cook 10 more minutes, or until tender. Heat the oven to 350°F.

Meanwhile, glaze the beef. Paint the mustard on the beef, sprinkle with cloves or ginger, then with the brown sugar. Bake for 15 to 20 minutes. Place the meat on a large serving platter and surround it with the vegetables. (Discard cooking water and spices.) Cut the meat across the grain.

Serves 6 to 8.

Red-Flannel Hash

This hash is a New England tradition. Leftover corned beef was often served as hash the next day. Serve it with fried eggs for breakfast or with a salad for supper.

    2 to 4 tablespoons vegetable oil
    1 cup chopped corned beef (about
        8 ounces)
    2 cups diced boiled potatoes
    2 large beets, cooked and chopped
    Salt and freshly ground black
        pepper

In a large frying pan, heat the oil over medium heat. Combine the corned beef, potatoes, and beets, spreading the mixture in the pan. Cook slowly until a nice brown crust forms on the bottom, approximately 20 to 30 minutes. Turn out the hash onto a plate and serve.

Serves 4.

Leather Britches Beans

Native Americans, and later the colonists, preserved green beans for winter use by drying them strung on a heavy thread. It can take a couple of weeks for the beans to dry this way. Since our modern "stringless" varieties of snap beans did not exist, people ate fresh or reconstituted cooked beans

whole with their fingers, holding on to the end of the bean and drawing it out across their teeth, to separate the meaty part from the string.

Serve with corn bread to soak up the juices.

    1 pound dried string beans
    1/4 pound ham, bacon, or salt pork
        (or some kind of game meat),
        cubed
    Salt and freshly ground black
        pepper
    1 small onion, diced (optional)

Wash the beans and place them in a bowl with 2 quarts of water. Soak for about 1 hour.

In a large pan or skillet, sauté the meat over medium heat for a few minutes. (Add some oil if the ham is lean, and onion if desired.) Add the beans and water, salt and pepper to taste, and simmer covered for 2 to 3 hours, or until the beans are tender. Check occasionally and add more water if there is less than 1/2 inch in the bottom of the pan.

Serves 6 to 8.

Fried Cucumbers

This recipe is from the *Old Sturbridge Village Cookbook;* according to Debra Friedman, early Americans seldom ate cucumbers raw.

When pared, cut [the cucumbers] in slices as thick as a dollar. Dry them with a cloth, and season with pepper and salt, and sprinkle them with flour. Have butter hot and lay them in. Fry of a light brown and send them to the table hot. They make a breakfast dish.

—Lydia Marie Child, *The American Frugal Housewife*, 1829

    4 pickling cucumbers (about 4 cups
        sliced)
    1 teaspoon salt
    1 teaspoon freshly ground black
        pepper
    1/3 cup all-purpose flour
    1/2 cup salted butter, divided

Cut the unpeeled cucumbers into 1/4-inch slices. Lay them on a towel to dry. Sprinkle them with salt and pepper. Lightly coat the seasoned cucumber slices with flour.

In a frying pan, melt part of the butter and fry the cucumbers over medium heat until light brown, about 10 to 15 minutes, turning them once. Transfer them to a heated serving dish and keep them warm. Add more butter to the frying pan and repeat the process until the remaining slices are done.

Serves 4 to 6.

Beerocks

Many of our "heirloom" recipes
came from English kitchens, but
our early American heritage draws
from other nationalities as well. This
old family recipe from Jan Blüm's
Grandma Bender originated in
Germany. These days, Jan uses a vege-
tarian filling instead of meat. As you
may notice, beerocks are very similar
to Russian *piroshkis*. Mustard is a good
accompaniment.

For the dough:

> 2 cups whole milk
>
> $1/2$ cup sugar
>
> $1/2$ cup vegetable oil
>
> 1 teaspoon salt
>
> 2 packages dried yeast
>
> 6 cups all-purpose flour

For the filling:

> $1/4$ cup vegetable oil
>
> 1 pound ground beef
>
> 2 large onions, chopped
>
> 1 large head cabbage, loosely
>   shredded
>
> A few leaves of kale or other leafy
>   green (optional)
>
> Salt and freshly ground black
>   pepper

To make the dough: In a saucepan
combine the milk, sugar, vegetable oil,
and salt. Heat the mixture until the
sugar has dissolved, but do not allow it
to boil. Cool the mixture to lukewarm.
Pour the milk mixture into the bowl of
a heavy-duty mixer with a dough hook
and stir the yeast into it. Add the flour

one cup at a the time and knead with the dough hook until the dough forms a ball. Turn the dough over in an oiled bowl, cover with plastic wrap, and let it rise in a warm place such as a 200°F. oven until it doubles in size, about 2 hours. Punch the dough down and let it rise for another hour.

While the dough is rising the second time, prepare the filling.

To make the filling: In a large skillet, heat the oil and brown the meat and onions over medium heat. Add the cabbage (and other greens if desired) and salt and pepper to taste. Cover and cook until crisp-tender. The skillet will be full at first, but the cabbage will shrink during cooking. Do not overcook. Take off the cover as soon as the cabbage has wilted, or the mixture will become too "juicy."

Heat the oven to 450°F and grease a cookie sheet with some vegetable oil.

After the dough has risen for the second time, place it on a floured board. Roll it out as thin as possible into a rectangle. Cut the dough into 8-inch squares. Spoon 2 to 3 tablespoons of the filling into the center of each square, being careful not to get any oil on the dough edges. Join the four corners of each square in the center and pinch each seam closed to make an envelope. Place the beerocks on the oiled cookie sheet, then turn them seam side down to oil both sides. Bake them for about 15 to 20 minutes, until they are nicely browned. Serve immediately.

Serves 16 as a side dish, 8 as a main course.

Baked Winter Squash with Maple Nut/Seed Butter

A wonderful complement to squash is a nut or seed butter. The rich flavors seem meant for each other. You can make your own nut or seed butter, and many types are available in natural food and specialty stores.

Only basic baking directions are given below; cooking times and the number of people served depend on the size and variety of squash.

> 2 acorn or other small squash (about 1¼ pounds each), or 1 medium squash (about 2½ pounds)
>
> 3 tablespoons salted butter
>
> 3 tablespoons nut or seed butter
>
> 3 tablespoons maple syrup

Heat the oven to 350°F.

Place the squash on a baking pan and cook for ¾ to 1½ hours, until soft. You may want to turn the squash a couple of times for more even cooking.

Cut the squash in half and remove the seeds (wash and save them to toast for snacks) and strings; if using one squash, cut the pieces again to make four servings. Return the squash to the baking pan, cut-sides up.

In a small saucepan, melt the butter, add nut or seed butter and syrup, and stir to mix. Spoon the butter mixture into the squash cavities and coat the surface of the squash. Return the squash to the oven for about 10 minutes to heat it through before serving.

Serves 4 as a side dish.

Succotash

Many Native American tribes combined beans with corn, thereby forming a complete protein. Succotash is one such combination dish, and it was made with fresh corn and shelled beans in midsummer and from reconstituted dried sweet corn and beans during the rest of the year. Here is my favorite recipe, made with fresh limas and corn. The variation with bacon would be a typical Southern version. See page 69 for tips on removing corn kernels from the cob.

3 tablespoons salted butter

1/2 onion, chopped

1/2 sweet pepper (green, red, or
    yellow)

2 cups fresh corn kernels
    (approximately 4 ears)

2 cups fresh shelled lima beans
    (approximately 1 pound)

Salt and freshly ground black
    pepper

Fresh hot pepper to taste, minced
    (optional)

1/3 cup milk or light cream
    (optional)

In a saucepan, melt the butter and sauté the onion (and hot pepper if desired) a few minutes to soften it. Add the sweet pepper and cook a few more minutes. Add the corn, beans, and 1 cup of water; cover; and simmer for about 15 minutes or until the limas are tender (large limas take longer). Add salt and pepper to taste (and add milk if desired) and serve.

Variation: Instead of using butter, cook 2 strips of bacon in a separate skillet until crisp. Remove the bacon and set it aside. Sauté the onion and pepper in the bacon fat. Put the sautéed onion and pepper in a saucepan with the corn, beans, and water and cook as above. Garnish with crumbled bits of the reserved bacon.

    Serves 4.

Corn Pudding

I modified this recipe after hearing the dish described by Debra Friedman at Old Sturbridge Village. She called it by its Colonial name, green corn pudding. The sweet corn kernels enveloped in rich custard is as big a treat today as it must have been years ago. See page 69 for tips on removing corn kernels from the cob. Serve the pudding as a side dish with meat and poultry or as a hearty lunch with a salad.

1 tablespoon salted butter

1 medium onion, finely chopped

3 cups fresh sweet corn kernels
(7 to 8 plump ears)

2 cups whole milk

6 large eggs, slightly beaten

Dash of freshly grated nutmeg

1 teaspoon sugar (optional)

Heat the oven to 350°F.

In a small nonstick pan, melt the butter over medium heat. Sauté the onion until translucent, about 7 minutes.

In a large bowl add the onion, corn, milk, eggs, and nutmeg (and sugar if the corn is not very sweet), and mix well. Pour the mixture into a small casserole or a 9-inch pottery pie dish. Bake for 1 hour, or until lightly brown and a knife inserted halfway into the center comes out clean.

Serves 6 as a side dish.

Stewed Tomatoes

For many years tomatoes were not eaten raw but were served cooked in a number of ways, including stewed. I've made this recipe for years—canning as many pints as I had time to produce. If you're planning to can this recipe, leave out the butter and add it when serving the tomatoes.

8 medium-size ripe tomatoes

1 tablespoon salted butter

1 teaspoon brown sugar

$1/4$ teaspoon dried thyme

$1/2$ teaspoon salt

Freshly ground black pepper

Peel and seed the tomatoes. In a medium saucepan, melt the butter and add the tomatoes, brown sugar, thyme, salt, and pepper. Simmer for 10 minutes over medium heat, or until the juice has reduced by about one third.

Serves 4.

Brussels Sprouts with Cream and Nuts

¹/₂ to 1 cup walnuts, hazelnuts, or
    roasted and peeled chestnuts
    (about 2 to 3 ounces)
1¹/₂ pounds (about 6 cups)
    brussels sprouts
2 tablespoons salted butter
³/₄ cup heavy cream (or substitute
    light cream)
Salt and freshly ground black
    pepper
Freshly ground nutmeg to taste

Bring about 3 cups of water to a boil, add the sprouts, and cook for 5 to 10 minutes, until barely tender. Drain the brussels sprouts. In a medium skillet, melt the butter and sauté the brussels sprouts over low heat for about 3 minutes. Add the cream and nuts; season to taste with salt, pepper, and nutmeg; and simmer, stirring, for 3 minutes.

Serves 6.

Brussels sprouts were one of the many vegetables that Thomas Jefferson introduced to America, and they quickly became popular. Be careful not to overcook them. They are wonderful combined with any kind of nuts.

If using walnuts or hazelnuts, first roast them at 300°F until fragrant but not brown, about 10 minutes. Rub the skins off the hazelnuts. Chop the nuts coarsely and set aside.

Wash the brussels sprouts thoroughly and cut a small X in the bottom of each one to ensure even cooking.

Creamed Onions

Fresh creamed onions have been a holiday staple for eons. While they are great with turkey, try them other times of the year with other roasts or as part of a vegetable medley.

24 small white onions, peeled
(about 1 1/4 pound)

4 tablespoons salted butter

3 tablespoons all-purpose flour

2 cups low-fat milk

1/2 teaspoon salt

1/4 teaspoon freshly ground black
pepper

1/4 teaspoon freshly grated nutmeg

Garnish: paprika

Boil the onions in 2 cups of water, uncovered, for 20 minutes, or until tender. The onions are done when you can insert a fork easily. Drain the cooking water into a bowl and reserve. You should have approximately 1/3 cup of cooking water left. Set the onions aside and keep them warm. In a heavy-bottomed saucepan, melt the butter and stir in the flour with a wire whisk. Cook this mixture over low heat for about 2 minutes, constantly stirring.

Add the reserved cooking water and continue to stir. Add the milk, and bring the sauce to a boil while whisking. Lower the heat, and simmer, stirring, for 3 to 5 minutes more. Add the salt, pepper, and nutmeg. Pour the sauce over the onions and sprinkle liberally with paprika. Serve immediately. Serves 4.

Candied Sweet Potatoes

3 large sweet potatoes (about 2
  pounds)

3 tablespoons salted butter

3 tablespoons dark brown sugar

1 tablespoon dark corn syrup

This recipe has its roots in the American South, but I grew up with it as part of our Massachusetts Thanksgiving feast and have continued the tradition in California for more than thirty years. Properly cooked sweet potatoes develop a chewy caramelized coating. For special occasions I double the recipe, using two large frying pans, since sweet potatoes are at their best just after they are cooked.

Wash the sweet potatoes and cut them in half lengthwise. Bring a large kettle of water to a boil, add the sweet potatoes, and cover. Boil for about 20 minutes, or until just tender. Keep an eye on them, as they usually get tender at an uneven rate. Drain the cooked sweet potatoes, let them cool slightly, and then peel them.

In a very large frying pan, melt the butter over low heat. Add the brown sugar and then drizzle the corn syrup over the melted butter and stir together.

Cut the sweet potato halves lengthwise and place them flat-side down in the pan in the butter mixture. Cook over medium to low heat for about 10 minutes, or until golden brown. Turn them over and cook for 5 to 10 more minutes, until both sides are golden. At this point you need to turn the pieces occasionally and watch carefully to prevent them from burning. Transfer them to a warm plate and serve immediately.

Serves 4.

Baked Beets

In days of old the large keeper beets, a winter staple, were roasted slowly over coals, intensifying their flavor and natural sweetness. Baking remains the best way for modern beet lovers to cook them; if you've never tried it, you'll be pleased with the results. Figure that one large (4- to 5-inch diameter) beet will feed two people. (Use the same formula for serving and cooking large carrots, as well.)

Scrub and trim the beets, but leave them whole. Set the greens aside.

Heat the oven to 300°F. Place the roots in a casserole or baking dish and cover securely. (Do not add water.) Bake them for at least 1 hour, or until just tender. Just before the roots are ready, wash the beet greens, slice them thin, and steam them for about 3 minutes, or until tender.

To serve, peel the beets, if so desired, and slice them; serve hot on a platter with the greens.

Serves 2 as a side dish.

Roast Parsnips

Roast parsnips are an honored tradition in England, where they have been a part of the holiday festivities. John Downey, chef and owner of Downey's in Santa Barbara, provided this recipe. Serve it with roast turkey, roast pork, or beef.

6 medium parsnips
4 tablespoons meat drippings
(turkey, pork, or beef) or butter

Heat the oven to 400°F.

Peel the parsnips and cut them into pieces approximately 3 inches by 3/4 inch. Blanch them in a pot of boiling water for 1 minute. Drain them well, spread them out, and pat dry. Heat an ovenproof skillet, add the meat drippings, letting them get very hot, add the parsnips, and sauté for a few minutes over high heat. Place them in the oven to finish cooking—about 30 minutes. Drain them and serve.

Variation: Roast the parsnips right in the meat pan after blanching them. They will be tastier but will hold more fat.

Serves 6.

Turnip Puree

John Downey offers this traditional way to prepare turnips, but you can prepare carrots and rutabagas the same way. He believes these wonderful old vegetables treated in this manner should receive more attention. Delicious!

> 1/4 cup salted butter
>
> 5 pounds turnips, well peeled and sliced (about 20 to 25 small to medium turnips)
>
> Salt and freshly ground white pepper
>
> 1 cup heavy cream

In a thick-bottomed pot with a tight-fitting lid, melt the butter with 2 table-spoons of water. Add the turnips and a little salt and white pepper. Simmer over very low heat, stirring occasionally, for 1 to 1 1/2 hours, until the turnips become very mushy. Remove the lid and allow the water to evaporate, but be careful not to burn the turnips. When they're fairly dry, remove them from the heat and let them cool. Pass the turnips through a food mill or a meat grinder. (A food processor is fine but may leave lumps.) If the mixture is too juicy and there are juices visible in the bottom of the pan, drain the puree in a conical strainer, saving the juices. Combine the juices with the cream in a saucepan and reduce the liquid over medium heat until quite thick. Add the turnip puree to the cream and warm it through; adjust the seasonings if necessary and serve.

Serves 6.

New Potatoes with Butter and Parsley

Boiled potatoes are classic Sunday dinner accompaniments to roast chicken, pork, and beef.

> 6 medium or 30 small boiling potatoes, red or white or both
>
> 2 tablespoons salted butter
>
> 1 1/2 tablespoons fresh minced parsley
>
> Salt and freshly ground black pepper

Wash the potatoes well, and cut any large ones into quarters or sixths. Keep small potatoes whole. (For a decorative presentation, remove a strip of skin around the middle.) Steam them for 15 to 20 minutes for medium potatoes, and for 5 to 10 minutes for small ones. In a skillet, melt the butter, add the parsley, salt, and pepper; and then add the potatoes. Stir the potatoes until coated, then transfer to a warm serving bowl.

Serves 6.

Carrot Pie

1 teaspoon cinnamon

$1/2$ teaspoon ginger

$1/4$ teaspoon freshly ground
    nutmeg

$1/8$ teaspoon allspice or cloves

3 eggs

1 unbaked 9-inch pie shell

Today Americans think of vegetable pies as being pumpkin or squash, traditionally enjoyed as holiday desserts. However, in Colonial days all vegetable pies, including carrot pie, were similarly spiced and were enjoyed as part of a large farm lunch or supper, not as dessert. Who knows, you may make this pie and start a new family tradition—pie for lunch.

$1^1/4$ pounds carrots

$3/4$ cup white or brown sugar

1 cup milk or cream

Wash the carrots and peel the skins if they are tough. Slice the carrots and steam them until tender. (You should have about 4 cups of sliced carrots.) Puree them in a blender or food processor.

Heat the oven to 425°F.

Add the remaining ingredients to the carrots in a mixing bowl and blend until smooth and evenly mixed. (You may have to do so in two batches, depending on the blender's capacity. If so, mix the batches together before pouring the puree into the pie shell.) Pour the puree into the pie shell. Bake for 15 minutes. Reduce heat to 350°F and bake for 45 more minutes, or until set. Let the pie cool for at least 30 minutes before serving.

Serves 6.

Rhubarb and Strawberry Cobbler

This traditional rhubarb cobbler is surprisingly light and creamy. Most early Americans would have only dreamed of the orange or lemon zest; few would have been able to get it.

For the filling:

6 to 8 stalks rhubarb, cut into
  $^1/_2$-inch pieces (about 3 cups)

$^2/_3$ cup sugar

1 tablespoon orange or lemon zest

1 tablespoon salted butter

1 tablespoon all-purpose flour

3 cups sliced strawberries

For the batter:

1$^3/_4$ cups flour

1 tablespoon baking powder

$^1/_2$ teaspoon salt

6 tablespoons salted butter, chilled

$^1/_2$ cup sugar plus 2 tablespoons,
  divided

$^3/_4$ cup half-and-half

2 tablespoons grated orange or
  lemon zest, divided

1 cup heavy cream whipped with 1
  tablespoon sugar (optional)

To make the filling: In a saucepan over medium heat, cook the rhubarb, sugar, and 1 tablespoon orange zest until the rhubarb begins to juice, about 2 minutes. Add the butter and flour and bring to a boil while stirring. Cook for about 1 minute. Add the sliced strawberries. Remove from heat and pour fruit mixture into a deep 10-inch pie dish.

To make the batter: Heat the oven to 425°F. In a large bowl, sift together the flour, baking powder, and salt. Cut in the butter into small pieces. With a fork or a pastry cutter, cut the chilled butter until the mixture resembles coarse crumbs. Add $^1/_2$ cup of the sugar and blend. Slowly incorporate the half-and-half with a fork. Spoon the dough over the fruit mixture in the pie dish. Mix 2 tablespoons sugar and the remaining orange zest and sprinkle it over the top. Bake for 25 to 30 minutes, or until golden brown. Cool slightly and serve with or without whipped cream.

Serves 6.

appendix A planting and maintenance

Covered in this section are the basics of planning a vegetable garden, preparing the soil, starting seeds, transplanting, fertilizing, composting, using floating row covers, rotating crops, mulching, watering and installing irrigation, and maintaining vegetables.

Planning Your Vegetable Garden

You can interplant a few heirloom vegetables among your ornamentals, or add them to your existing vegetable garden. If you have no vegetable garden, then you need to design one. The first step in planning your vegetable garden is choosing a suitable site. Most chefs recommend locating the edible garden as close to the kitchen as possible, and I heartily agree. Beyond that, the majority of vegetables need at least six hours of sun (eight is better)—except in warm, humid areas, where afternoon or some filtered shade is best—and good drainage. Annual vegetables need fairly rich soil with lots of added organic matter. They can be planted in rows in a bed by themselves—as part of the classic vegetable garden, say—but many of them, especially amaranth, peppers, kale, okra, lettuce, rhubarb, and summer squash, are beautiful and work well interplanted in a flower bed with annual flowers, most of which need the same conditions. In addition, most vegetables can be grown in containers or in large planter boxes.

Once you've decided on where you are going to plant, it's time to choose your vegetables. Your major consideration is, of course, what flavors you enjoy using in the kitchen. With this in mind, look for species and varieties that grow well in your climate. As a rule, gardeners in northern climates and high elevations look for vegetables that tolerate cool and/or short summer conditions. Many vegetable varieties bred for short seasons and most salad greens are great for these conditions. Gardeners in hot, humid areas require plants that tolerate diseases well and need to consider carefully choosing heat-tolerant vegetables.

The USDA Plant Hardiness Zone Map has grouped eleven zones according to winter lows, a help in choosing perennial plants but of only limited use for annual vegetables. The new *Sunset National Garden Book,* published by Sunset Books, gives much more useful climatic information; it divides the continent into forty-five growing zones. Several regional maps describe the temperature ranges and growing season in much detail. The maps are an integral part of this information-packed resource. Of additional interest to the vegetable gardener is the AHS Plant Heat-Zone Map, published by the American Horticultural Society. The heat map details twelve zones and lists the average number of days each year when a given area experiences temperatures of 86°F or higher—the temperature at which many plants, including peas and most salad greens, begin to suffer physiological damage. In "An Encyclopedia of Heirloom Vegetables" (page 21) I indicate which varieties have a low tolerance for high temperatures and those that grow well in hot weather. See the bibliography for information on obtaining the heat map.

In addition to analyzing your climate, knowing what type of soil a particular vegetable needs is equally important. Consider how well your soil drains: is it rich with organic matter and fertility? Poor soil with bad drainage? Is it so sandy that few plants grow well? Find out too what your soil pH is. Nurseries have kits to test your soil's pH, and University Extension Services can lead you to sources of soil tests and soil experts. As a rule, rainy climates have acidic soil that needs the pH raised, and arid climates have fairly neutral or alkaline soil that needs extra organic matter to lower the pH. Most vegetables grow best in soil with a pH of about 6.5—in other words, slightly acidic. Soil that is below 6 ties up phosphorus, potassium, and calcium, making them unavailable to plants; soil with a pH much over 6.5 ties up iron and zinc.

Furthermore, is there hardpan under your garden that prevents roots from penetrating the soil, or water from draining? This is a fairly common problem in areas of heavy clay, especially in many parts of the Southwest with caliche soils—a very alkaline clay. You need answers to these basic questions before you proceed because annual vegetables need to grow fast and with little stress to be tender and mild.

Vegetable plants do best with good drainage. Their roots need air, and if the soil stays waterlogged for long, roots suffocate or are prone to root rot. If you are unsure how well a particular area in your garden drains, dig a hole where you plan to put your garden, about 10 inches deep and 10 inches across, and fill it with water. The next day fill it again—if it still has water in it eight to ten hours later, you need to find another place in the garden that will drain much faster, amend your soil with much organic matter and mound it up at least 6 to 8 inches above the ground level, or grow your vegetables in containers.

The last consideration is how large a garden you are planning. A few hundred square feet of heirloom vegetables like beans, beets, carrots, onions, and peppers, plus a small bed of heirloom lettuces, would give you many a delectable meal. If you want to get more involved and plant a large garden that might also include heirloom potatoes and broccoli during the cool season, or later the warm weather crops of indeterminate tomatoes, corn, and zucchini, you need more space (an area of at least 500 square feet would be ideal). Even more space will be needed for melons, large winter squashes, or pumpkins to provide enough vegetables for a family of four. In any case, the area can be rectangular, square, or free-form.

A garden of a few hundred square feet or more needs a path or two and the soil to be arranged in beds. Paths through any garden should be at least 3 feet across to provide ample room for walking and using a wheelbarrow, and beds should generally be limited to 5 feet across, as that is the average distance a person can reach into the bed to harvest or pull weeds from both sides. Protection too is often needed, so consider putting a fence or wall around the garden to give it a stronger design and to keep out rabbits, woodchucks, and the resident dog. Assuming you have chosen a nice sunny area, selected a design, and determined that your soil drains properly, you are ready to prepare the soil.

Installing a Vegetable Garden

Preparing the Soil

To prepare the soil for a new vegetable garden, first remove large rocks and weeds. Dig out any perennial weeds, especially perennial grasses like Bermuda and quack grass. You need to sift and closely examine each shovel-full for every little piece of their roots, or they will regrow with a vengeance. If you are taking up part of a lawn, the sod needs to be removed. If it is a small area, this can be done with a flat spade. Removing large sections, though, warrants renting a sod cutter. Next, when the soil is not too wet, spade over the area. Most vegetables are heavy feeders, and few soils support them without being supplemented with much organic matter and nutrients. The big three nutrients are nitrogen (N), phosphorus (P), and potassium (K)—the ones most frequently found in fertilizers. Calcium, magnesium, and sulfur are also important plant nutrients, and plants need a number of trace minerals for healthy growth, among them iron, zinc, boron, copper, and manganese. A soil test is the best way to see what your soil needs. In general, most soils benefit from at least an application of an organic nitrogen fertilizer. While it's hard to say what your soil needs without a test, the following gives you a rough idea of how much you need per 100 square feet of average soil: for nitrogen apply blood meal at 2 pounds, or fish meal at $2^{1/4}$ pounds; for phosphorus apply 2 pounds bonemeal; for potassium apply kelp meal according to the package, or in acidic soils $1^{1/2}$ pounds of hard wood ashes. Kelp meal also provides most trace minerals. (The addition of so many nutrients will not be needed in subsequent years if composting and mulching are practiced, especially if you rotate your crops and use cover crops.)

After the area has been spaded up, cover it with 4 or 5 inches of compost and an inch or two of well-aged manure. Add a few more inches of compost if you live in a hot, humid climate where heat burns the compost at an accelerated rate, or if you have very alkaline, very sandy, or very heavy clay soil. Since most vegetables grow best in a neutral soil, add lime at this point if a soil test indicates that your soil is acidic. Follow the directions on the package. Add fertilizers by sprinkling them over the soil. Incorporate all the ingredients thoroughly by turning the soil over with a spade, working the amendments into the top 8 to 12 inches. If your garden is large or the soil is very hard to work, you might use a rototiller. (When you put in a garden for the first time, a rototiller can be very helpful. However, research has shown that continued use of tillers is hard on soil structure and quickly burns up valuable organic matter if used regularly.)

Finally, grade and rake the area. You are now ready to form the beds and paths. Because of all the added materials, the beds will now be elevated above the paths—which further helps drainage. Slope the sides of the beds so that loose soil will not be easily washed or knocked onto the paths. Some gardeners add a brick or wood edging to outline the beds. Some sort of gravel, brick, stone, or mulch is needed on the paths to forestall weed growth and to prevent your feet from getting wet and muddy.

The last task before planting your garden is providing support for vining crops like pole beans and tomatoes. There are many types of supports, from simple stakes to elaborate wire cages; whichever you choose, install them before you plant.

Starting from Seeds

You can grow all annual vegetables from seeds. They can be started indoors in flats or other well-drained containers, outdoors in a cold frame, or, depending on the time of year, directly in the garden. When I start annual vegetables inside, I seed them in either plastic pony packs that I recycle from the nursery or in Styrofoam compartmentalized containers variously called plugs or speedling trays (available from mail-order garden-supply houses). Whatever type of container you use, the soil depth should be 2 to 3 inches deep. Any shallower dries out too fast, and deeper soil is usually a waste of seed-starting soil and water.

Starting seeds inside gives your seedlings a safe start away from slugs and birds. It also allows gardeners in cold or hot climates to get a jump on the season. Many vegetables can be started four to six weeks before the last expected frost date and then transplanted out into the garden as soon as the soil can be worked. Furthermore, some vegetables are sensitive to high temperatures; by starting them inside in mid- or late summer, the seeds will germinate and the seedlings will get a good start and be ready to be transplanted outside in early fall, when the weather has started to cool.

The cultural needs of seeds vary widely among species; still, some basic rules apply to most seeding procedures. First, whether starting seeds in the ground or in a container, make sure you have loose, water-retentive soil that drains well. Good drainage is important because seeds can get waterlogged, and too much water can lead to "damping off," a fungal disease that kills seedlings at the soil line. Commercial starting mixes are usually best since they have been sterilized to remove weed seeds; however, the quality varies greatly from brand to brand, and I find most lack enough nitrogen, so I water with a weak solution of fish emulsion when I plant the seeds, and again a week or so later.

Smooth the soil surface and plant the seeds at the recommended depth. Information on seed depth is included in An Encyclopedia of Heirloom Vegetables (page 21) as well as on the back of most seed packages. Pat down the seeds, and water carefully to make the seed bed moist but not soggy. Mark the name of the plant and variety and the date of seeding on a plastic or wooden label and place it at the head of the row. When starting seeds outside, protect the seed bed with either floating row covers or bird netting to keep out critters. If slugs and snails are a problem, circle the area with hardwood ashes or diatomaceous earth to keep them away and go out at night with a flashlight to catch any that cross the barrier. If you are starting seeds in containers, put the seedling tray in a warm, but not hot, place to help seeds germinate more quickly.

When starting seeds inside, once they have germinated, it's imperative that they immediately be given a quality source of light; otherwise, the new seedlings will be spindly and pale. A greenhouse, sunporch, or south-facing window with no overhang will suffice, provided it is warm. If one is not available, use fluorescent lights, which are available from home-supply stores or from specialty mail-order houses. The lights are hung just above the plants for maximum light (no farther than 3 or 4 inches away, at most) and moved up as the plants get taller. Another option I use if the weather is above 60°F is to put my seedling trays outside on a table in the sun and protect them with bird netting during the day, bringing them in at night.

Once seedlings are up, keep them moist and, if you have seeded thickly and have crowded plants, thin some out. It's less damaging to do so with small scissors. Cut the little plants out, leaving the remaining seedlings an inch or so apart. Do not transplant your seedlings until they have their second set of true leaves (the first leaves that sprout from a seed are called seed leaves and usually look different from the later true leaves). If the seedlings are tender, wait until all danger of frost is past before you set them out. In fact, don't put heat-loving tomatoes and peppers out until the weather has thoroughly warmed up and is stable. Young plants started indoors should be "hardened off" before they are planted in the garden—that is, they should be put outside in a sheltered place for a few days in their containers to let them get used to the differences in temperature, humidity, and air movement outside. A cold frame is perfect for hardening off plants.

Transplanting

I generally start my annual vegetables from seeds and then transplant them outside. Occasionally I buy transplants from local nurseries. Before setting transplants out in the garden, check to see if a mat of roots has formed at the bottom of the root ball. I remove it or open it up so the roots won't continue to grow in a tangled mass. I set the plant in the ground at the same height as it was in the container, pat the plant in place gently by hand, and water each plant in well to remove air bubbles. I space plants so that they won't be crowded once they mature; when vegetables grow too close together, they become prone to rot diseases and mildew. If I'm planting on a very hot day or the transplants have been in a protected greenhouse, I shade them with a shingle or such, placed on the sunny side of the plants. I then install my irrigation ooze tubing (see "Watering and Irrigation Systems" (page 95) for more information)

and mulch with a few inches of organic matter. I keep the transplants moist but not soggy for the first few weeks.

Floating Row Covers

Among the most valuable tools for plant protection in the vegetable garden are floating row covers made of lightweight spun-bond polyester or polypropylene fabric. They are laid directly over the plants, where they "float" in place. These covers protect plants against cold weather and pests.

If used correctly, row covers are a most effective pest control for cucumber, asparagus, bean, and potato beetles; squash bugs and vine borers; cabbage worms; leafhoppers; onion maggots; aphids; and leaf miners. The most lightweight covers, usually called summer-weight or insect barriers because they have little heat buildup, can be used throughout the season for insect control in all but the hottest climates. They cut down on 10 percent of the sunlight, which is seldom a problem unless your garden is shady. Heavier versions, sometimes called garden covers under trade names like Reemay, and Tufbell, variously cut down from 15 percent to 50 percent of the sunlight and guard against pests, but they also raise the temperature underneath from 2 to 7°F, usually enough to protect early and late crops from frost or to add warmth for heat-loving crops in cool-summer areas.

In addition to effectively protecting plants from cold weather and many pests, there are numerous other advantages to using floating row covers:

- The stronger ones protect plants from most songbirds, though not from crafty squirrels and blue jays.
- They raise the humidity around plants, a bonus in arid climates, but a problem with some crops in humid climates.
- They protect young seedlings from sunburn in summer and in high-altitude gardens.

There are a few limitations to consider:

- These covers keep out pollinating bees and must be removed when squash, melons, and cucumbers are in production.
- They are not attractive enough to use over most flower beds and in decorative settings. In fact, they make the garden look like a sorority slumber party.
- Many of the fabrics last only a year and then start to deteriorate. (I use tattered small pieces to cover containers, in the bottoms of containers to keep out slugs, etc.)
- Row covers use petroleum products and eventually end up in the landfill.
- In very windy areas, the tunnels and floating row covers are apt to be blown away or become shredded.
- The heavyweight versions cut down on much light and are useful only to help raise temperatures when frost threatens.

Rolls of the fabric, from 5 to 10 feet wide and up to 100 feet long, can be purchased from local nurseries or ordered from garden-supply catalogs. As a rule, you have a wider selection of materials and sizes from mail-order sources.

Before you apply your row cover, fully prepare the bed and make sure it's free of eggs, larvae, and adult pests. (For example, if instead of rotating your crops, you follow onions with onions in the same bed, you are apt to have larvae of the onion root maggot trapped under the cover—with their favorite food and safe from predators!) Then install drip irrigation if you are using it, plant your crop, and mulch (if appropriate). There are two ways to lay a row cover: either directly on the plants or stretched over wire hoops. Laying the cover directly on the plants is the easiest method.

However, laying it over hoops has the advantage that it is easier to check under the row cover, and some plants are sensitive to abrasion if the wind whips the cover around, causing the tips of the plants to turn brown. When you lay the fiber directly on the plants, leave some slack so plants have room to grow. For both methods, secure the edges completely with bricks, rocks, old pieces of lumber, bent wire hangers or u-shaped metal pins sold for this purpose.

To avoid pitfalls, it's critical to check under the row covers from time to time. Check soil moisture; the fibers sometimes shed rain and overhead irrigation water. Check as well for weeds; the protective fiber aids their growth too. And most important, check for any insect pests that may have been trapped inside.

Maintaining the Vegetable Garden

The backbone of appropriate maintenance is a knowledge of your soil and weather, an ability to recognize basic water- and nutrient-deficiency symptoms, and a familiarity with the plants you grow.

Annual vegetables are growing machines. As a rule, they need to grow rapidly with few interruptions so they produce well and have few pest problems. Once the plants are in the ground, continually monitoring for nutrient deficiencies, drought, and pests can head off problems. Keep the beds weeded because weeds compete for moisture and nutrients. In normal soil, most vegetables need supplemental nitrogen fertilizer. Fish emulsion and fish meal, blood meal, and chicken manure all have their virtues. Sandy or problem soils may need more nutrients to provide potassium and trace minerals, if so kelp meal or emulsions can be added to the nitrogen sources mentioned above, or apply a packaged balanced organic vegetable fertilizer. For more specific information on fertilizing, see the individual entries in An Encyclopedia of Heirloom Vegetables (page 21).

Weeding

Weeding is needed to make sure unwanted plants don't compete with and overpower your vegetables. A good small triangular hoe will help you weed a small garden if you start when the weeds are young and easily hoed. If you allow the weeds to get large, a session of hand pulling is needed. Applying a mulch is a great way to cut down on weeds; however, if you have a big problem with slugs in your garden, the mulch gives them more places to hide. Another means of controlling weeds, namely annual weeds like crabgrass, pigweed, and quack grass, is a new organic preemergence herbicide made from corn gluten called Concern Weed Prevention Plus. This gluten meal inhibits the tiny feeder roots of germinating weed seeds, so they wither and die. It does not kill existing weeds. Obviously, if you use it among new seedlings or in seed beds, it kills them too, so it is only useful in areas away from very young plants.

Mulching

Mulching can save the gardener time, effort, and water. A mulch reduces moisture loss, prevents erosion, controls weeds, minimizes soil compaction, and moderates soil temperature. When the mulch is an organic material, it adds nutrients and organic matter to the soil as it decomposes, making heavy clay more porous and helping sandy soil retain moisture. Mulches are often attractive additions to the garden as well. Applying a few inches of organic matter every spring is necessary in most vegetable gardens to keep them healthy. Mulch with compost from your compost pile, pine needles, composted sawdust, straw, or one of the many agricultural by-products like rice hulls or apple or grape pomace.

Compost

Compost is the humus-rich result of the decomposition of organic matter, such as leaves and garden trimmings. The objective of maintaining a composting system is to speed up decomposition and centralize the material so you can gather it up and spread it where it will do the most good. Compost's benefits include providing nutri-

ents to plants in a slow-release, balanced fashion; helping break up clay soil; aiding sandy soil to retain moisture; and correcting pH problems. On top of that, compost is free, it can be made at home, and it is an excellent way to recycle our yard and kitchen "wastes." Compost can be used as a soil additive or a mulch.

There need be no great mystique about composting. To create the environment needed by the decay-causing microorganisms that do all the work, just include the following four ingredients, mixed well: three or four parts "brown" material high in carbon, such as dry leaves, dry grass, or even shredded black-and-white newspaper; one part "green" material high in nitrogen, such as fresh grass clippings, fresh garden trimmings, barnyard manure, or kitchen trimmings like pea pods and carrot tops; water in moderate amounts, so that the mixture is moist but not soggy; and air to supply oxygen to the microorganisms. Bury the kitchen trimmings within the pile, so as not to attract flies. Cut up any large pieces of material. Exclude weeds that have gone to seed, because they can lead to the growth of those weeds in the garden. Do not add meat, fat, diseased plants, woody branches, or cat or dog manure.

I don't stress myself about the proper proportions of compost materials, as long as I have a fairly good mix of materials from the garden. If the decomposition is too slow, it is usually because the pile has too much brown material, is too dry, or needs air. If the pile smells, there is too much green material or it is too wet. To speed up decomposition, I often chop or shred the materials before adding them to the pile and I may turn the pile occasionally to get

additional oxygen to all parts. During decomposition, the materials can become quite hot and steamy, which is great; however, it is not mandatory that the compost become extremely hot.

You can make compost in a simple pile, in wire or wood bins, or in rather expensive containers. The size should be about 3 feet high, wide, and tall for the most efficient decomposition and so the pile is easily workable. It can be up to 5 feet by 5 feet, but it then becomes harder to manage. In a rainy climate it's a good idea to have a cover for the compost. I like to use three bins. I collect the compost materials in one bin, have a working bin, and when that bin is full, I turn the contents into the last bin, where it finishes its decomposition. I sift the finished compost into empty garbage cans so it does not leach its nutrients into the soil. The empty bin is then ready to fill up again.

Crop Rotation

Rotating crops in an edible garden has been practiced for centuries. It's done for two reasons: to help prevent diseases and pests and to prevent depletion of nutrients from the soil, as some crops add nutrients and others take them away.

To rotate crops, you must know what plants are in which families, since plants in the same families are often prone to the same diseases and pests and deplete the same nutrients.

The following is a short list of related vegetables.

Goosefoot family (*Chenopodiaceae*)— includes beets, chard, orach, spinach

Cucumber family (gourd) (*Cucurbitaceae*)—includes cucumbers, gourds, melons, summer squash, winter squash, pumpkins

Lily family (onion) (*Liliaceae*)—includes asparagus, chives, garlic, leeks, onions, Oriental chives, shallots

Mint family (*Lamiaceae*)—includes basil, mints, oregano, rosemary, sages, summer savory, thymes

Mustard family (cabbage) (*Brassicaceae*)—includes arugula, broccoli, cabbages, cauliflower, collards, cresses, kale, kohlrabi, komatsuna, mizuna, mustards, radishes, turnips

Nightshade family (*Solanaceae*)—includes eggplants, peppers, potatoes, tomatillos, tomatoes

Parsley family (carrot) (*Apiaceae*)— includes carrots, celeriac, celery, chervil, coriander (cilantro), dill, fennel, lovage, parsley, parsnips

Pea family (legumes) (*Fabaceae*)— includes beans, cowpeas, fava beans, lima beans, peanuts, peas, runner beans, soybeans, sugar peas

Sunflower family (daisy) (*Asteraceae*)— includes artichokes, calendulas, celtuce, chicories, dandelions, endives, lettuces, marigolds, tarragon

The object is to avoid growing members of the same family in the same spot year after year. For example: cabbage, a member of the mustard family, should not be followed by radishes, a member of the same family, as they are both prone to flea beetles and the flea beetle's eggs will be in the soil ready to hatch and attack the radishes. Tomatoes should not follow eggplants, as they are both prone to fusarium wilt.

Crop rotation is also practiced to help keep the soil healthy. One family, namely the pea family (legumes), which includes not only peas and beans but also clovers and alfalfa, adds nitrogen to the soil. In contrast, most members of the mustard (cabbage) family deplete the soil of nitrogen. Other heavy feeders are members of the nightshade and cucumber families. Because most vegetables deplete the soil, knowledgeable gardeners not only rotate their beds with vegetables from different families; they also include an occasional cover crop of clover or alfalfa and other soil benefactors like buckwheat and vetch to add what's called green manure. After growing for a few months, these crops are turned under and provide extra organic matter and many nutrients, help stop the pest cycle, and attract beneficial insects. Some cover crops (like rye) are grown over the winter to control soil erosion. The seeds of all sorts of cover crops are available from farm suppliers and specialty seed companies. I've been able to give only the basics on this subject; for more information, see Shepherd Ogden's *Step by Step Organic Vegetable Gardening* and some of the other basic gardening texts recommended in the bibliography.

Watering and Irrigation Systems

Even gardeners who live in rainy climates may need to do supplemental watering at specific times during the growing season. Therefore, most gardeners need some sort of supplemental watering system and a knowledge of water management.

There is no easy formula for determining the correct amount or frequency of watering. Proper watering takes experience and observation. In addition to the specific watering needs of individual plants, the amount of watering needed depends on soil type, wind conditions, and air temperature. To water properly, you must learn how to recognize water-stress symptoms (often a dulling of foliage color as well as the better-known symptoms of drooping leaves and wilting), how much to water (too much is as bad as too little), and how to water. Some general rules are

1. Water deeply. Except for seed beds, most plants need infrequent deep watering rather than frequent light sprinkling.

2. To ensure proper absorption, apply water at a rate slow enough to prevent runoff.

3. Do not use overhead watering systems when the wind is blowing.

4. Try to water early in the morning so that foliage will have time to dry off before nightfall, thus preventing some disease problems. In addition, because of the cooler temperature, less water is lost to evaporation.

5. Test your watering system occasionally to make sure it is covering the area evenly.

6. Use methods and tools that conserve water. When using a hose, a pistol-grip nozzle will shut off the water while you move from one container or planting bed to another. Soaker hoses, made of either canvas or recycled tires, and other ooze and drip irrigation systems apply water slowly and use water more efficiently than do overhead systems.

Drip, or the related ooze/trickle, irrigation systems are advisable wherever feasible, and most gardens are well-suited to them. Drip systems deliver water a drop at a time through spaghettilike emitter tubes or plastic pipe with emitters that drip water right onto the root zone of each plant. Because of the time and effort involved in installing one or two emitters per plant, these systems work best for permanent plantings such as in rose beds, with rows of daylilies and lavender say, or with trees and shrubs. These lines require continual maintenance to make sure the individual emitters are not clogged.

Other similar systems, called ooze systems, deliver water through either holes made every 6 or 12 inches along solid flexible tubing or ooze along the entire porous hose. Neither system is as prone to clogging as are the emitters. The solid type is made of plastic and is often called laser tubing. It is pressure compensated, which means the flow of water is even throughout the length of the tubing. The high quality brands have a built-in mechanism to minimize clogging and are made of tubing that will not expand in hot weather and, consequently, pop off its fittings. (Some of the inexpensive drip irrigation kits can make you crazy!) The porous hose types are made from recycled tires and come in two sizes—a standard hose diameter of 1 inch, great for shrubs and trees planted in a row, and $1/4$ inch tubing that can be snaked around beds of small plants. Neither are pressure compensated, which means the plants nearest the source of water get more water than those at the end of the line. It also means they will not work well if there is any slope. All types of drip emitter and ooze systems are installed after the plants are in the ground, and are held in place with ground staples. To install any drip or ooze system you must also install an anti-siphon valve at the water source to prevent dirty garden water from being drawn up into the house's drinking water. Further, a filter is needed to prevent debris from clogging the emitters. To set up the system, connect 1-inch distribution tubing to the water source and lay it out around the perimeter of the garden. Then connect smaller diameter drip and ooze lines to this. As you can see, installing these systems requires some thought and time. You can order these systems from either a specialty mail-order garden or irrigation source or visit your local plumbing store. I find the latter to be the best solution for all my irrigation problems. Over the years I've found that plumbing supply stores offer professional-quality supplies, usually for less money than the so-called inexpensive kits available in home-supply stores and some nurseries. In addition to quality materials, there are professionals there to help you lay out an irrigation design that is tailored to your garden. Whether you choose an emitter or an ooze system, when you go to buy your tubing, be prepared by bringing a rough drawing of the area to be irrigated—with dimensions, the location of the water source and any slopes, and, if possible, the water pressure at your water source. Let the professionals walk you through the steps and help pick out supplies that best fit your site.

Problems aside, all forms of drip irrigation are more efficient than furrow or standard overhead watering in delivering water to its precise destination and are well worth considering. They deliver water slowly, so it doesn't run off; they also water deeply, which encourages deep rooting. Drip irrigation also eliminates many disease problems, and because so little of the soil surface is moist, there are fewer weeds. Finally, they have the potential to waste a lot less water.

appendix B pest and disease control

The following sections cover a large number of pests and diseases. An individual gardener, however, will encounter few such problems in a lifetime of gardening. Good garden planning, good hygiene, and an awareness of major symptoms will keep problems to a minimum and give you many hours to enjoy your garden and feast on its bounty.

There are some spoilers, though, which sometimes need control. For years controls were presented as a list of critters and diseases, followed by the newest and best chemical to control them. But times have changed, and we now know that chasing the latest chemical to fortify our arsenal is a bit like chasing our tail. That's because most pesticides, both insecticides and fungicides, kill beneficial insects as well as the pests; therefore, the more we spray, the more we are forced to spray. Nowadays, we've learned that successful pest control focuses on prevention, plus beefing up the natural ecosystem so beneficial insects are on pest patrol. How does that translate to pest control for the vegetable garden directly?

1. When possible, seek resistant varieties—for example, in cold, wet weather choose lettuce varieties resistant to downy mildew, and if fungal diseases are a problem in your garden, select disease-resistant varieties of tomatoes.

2. Use mechanical means to prevent insect pests from damaging the plants. For example, cover young squash or potato plants with floating row covers to keep away squash borers and flea beetles; sprinkle wood ashes around plants to prevent cabbage root maggot and slug damage; and put cardboard collars around young tomato, pepper, cabbage, and squash seedlings to prevent cutworms from destroying them.

3. Clean up diseased foliage and dispose of it in the garbage to cut down on the cycle of infection.

4. Rotate your crops so that plants from the same family are not planted in the same place for two consecutive seasons.

5. Encourage and provide food for beneficial insects. In the vegetable garden this translates to letting a few selected vegetables go to flower and growing flowering herbs and ornamentals to provide a season-long source of nectar and pollen for beneficial insects.

Beneficial Insects

In a nutshell, few insects are potential problems; most are either neutral or beneficial to the gardener. Given the chance, the beneficials do much of your insect control for you, provided that you don't use pesticides, as pesticides are apt to kill the beneficial insects as well as the problem insects. Like predatory lions stalking zebra, predatory ladybugs (lady beetles) or lacewing larvae hunt and eat aphids that might be attracted to your lettuce, say. Or a mini-wasp parasitoid will lay eggs in the aphids. If you spray those aphids, even with a so-called benign pesticide such as insecticidal soap or pyrethrum, you'll kill off the ladybugs, lacewings, and that baby parasitoid wasp too. Most insecticides are broad spectrum, which means that they kill insects indiscriminately, not just the pests. In my opinion, organic gardeners who regularly use organic broad-spectrum insecticides have missed this point. While it is true they are using an "organic" pesticide, they may actually be eliminating a truly organic means of control, the beneficial insects.

Unfortunately, many gardeners are not aware of the benefits of the predator-prey relationship and are not able to recognize beneficial insects. The following sections will help you identify both helpful and pest organisms. A more detailed aid for identifying insects is *Rodale's Color Handbook of Garden Insects*, by Anna Carr. A hand lens is an invaluable and inexpensive tool that will also help you identify the insects in your garden.

Predators and Parasitoids

Insects that feed on other insects are divided into two types, the predators and the parasitoids. Predators are mobile. They stalk plants looking for such plant feeders as aphids and mites. Parasitoids, on the other hand, are insects that develop in or on the bodies, pupae, or eggs of other host insects. Most parasitoids are minute wasps or flies whose larvae (young stages) eat other insects from within. Some of the wasps are so small, they can develop within an aphid or an insect egg. Or one parasitoid egg can divide into several identical cells, each developing into identical miniwasp larvae, which then can kill an entire caterpillar. Though nearly invisible to most gardeners, parasitoids are the most specific and effective means of insect control.

The predator-and-prey relationship can be a fairly stable situation; when the natural system is working properly, pest insects inhabiting the garden along with the predators and parasitoids seldom become a problem. Sometimes, though, the system breaks down. For example, a number of imported pests have taken hold in this country. Unfortunately, when such organisms were brought here, their natural predators did not accompany them. Four pesky examples are Japanese beetles, the European brown snail, the white cabbage butterfly, and flea beetles. None of these organisms has natural enemies in this country that provide sufficient controls. Where they occur, it is sometimes necessary to use physical means or selective pesticides that kill only the problem insect. Weather extremes sometime produce imbalances as well. For example, long stretches of hot, dry weather favor grasshoppers that invade vegetable gardens, because the diseases that keep them in check are more prevalent under moist conditions. There are other situations in which the predator-prey relationship gets out of balance because many gardening practices inadvertently work in favor of the pests. For example, when gardeners spray with broad-spectrum pesticides regularly, not all the insects in the garden are killed—and since predators and parasitoids generally reproduce more slowly than do the pests, regular spraying usually tips the balance in favor of the pests. Further, all too often the average yard has few plants that produce nectar for beneficial insects; instead it is filled with grass and shrubs, so that when a few squash plants and a row of lettuces are put in, the new plants attract the aphids but not the beneficials. Being aware of the effect of these practices will help you create a vegetable garden that is relatively free of many pest problems.

Attracting Beneficial Insects

Besides reducing your use of pesticides, the key to keeping a healthy balance in your garden is providing a diversity of plants, including plenty of nectar- and pollen-producing plants. Nectar is the primary food of the adult stage and some larval stages of many beneficial insects. Interplanting your vegetables with flowers and numerous herbs helps attract them. Ornamentals, like species zinnias, marigolds, alyssum, and yarrow, provide many flowers over a long season and are shallow enough for insects to reach the nectar. Large, dense flowers like tea roses and dahlias are useless as their nectar is out of reach. A number of the herbs are rich nectar sources, including fennel, dill, anise, chervil, oregano, thyme, and parsley. Allowing a few of your heirloom vegetables like broccoli, carrots, and kale, in particular, to go to flower is helpful because their tiny flowers full of nectar and pollen are just what many of the beneficial insects need.

Following are a few of the predatory and parasitoid insects that are helpful in the garden. Their preservation and protection should be a major goal of your pest-control strategy.

Ground beetles and their larvae are all predators. Most adult ground beetles are fairly large black beetles that scurry out from under plants or containers when you disturb them. Their favorite foods are soft-bodied larvae like Colorado potato beetle larvae and root maggots (root maggots eat cabbage family plants); some ground beetles even eat snails and slugs. If supplied with an undisturbed place to live, like your compost area or groupings of perennial plantings, ground beetles will be long-lived residents of your garden.

Lacewings are one of the most effective insect predators in the home garden. They are small green or brown gossamer-winged insects that in their adult stage eat flower nectar, pollen, aphid honeydew, and sometimes aphids and mealybugs. In the larval stage they look like little tan alligators. Called aphid lions, the larvae are fierce predators of aphids, mites, and whiteflies—all occasional pests that suck plant sap. If you are having problems with sucking insects in your garden, consider purchasing lacewing eggs or larvae mail-order to jump-start your lacewing population. Remember to plant lots of nectar plants to keep the population going from year to year.

Lady beetles (ladybugs) are the best known of the beneficial garden insects. Actually, there are about four hundred species of lady beetles in North America alone. They come in a variety of colors and markings in addition to the familiar red with black spots, but they are never green. Lady beetles and their fierce-looking alligator-shaped larvae eat copious amounts of aphids and other small insects.

Spiders are close relatives of insects. There are hundreds of species, and they are some of the most effective predators of a great range of pest insects.

Syrphid flies (also called flowerflies or hover flies) look like small bees hovering over flowers, but they have only two wings. Most have yellow and black stripes on their body. Their larvae are small green maggots that inhabit leaves, eating small sucking insects and mites.

Wasps are a large family of insects with transparent wings. Unfortunately, the few large wasps that sting have given wasps a bad name. In fact, all wasps are either insect predators or parasitoids. The miniwasps are usually parasitoids, and the adult female lays her eggs in such insects as aphids, whitefly larvae, and caterpillars—and the developing wasp larvae devour the host. These miniature wasps are also available for purchase from insectaries and are especially effective when released in greenhouses.

Pests

The following pests are sometimes a problem in the vegetable garden.

Aphids are soft-bodied, small, green, black, pink, or gray insects that produce many generations in one season. They suck plant juices and exude honeydew. Sometimes leaves under the aphids turn black from a secondary mold growing on the nutrient-rich honeydew. Aphids are primarily a problem on cabbages, broccoli, beans, lettuces, peas, and tomatoes. Aphid populations can build up, especially in the spring before beneficial insects are present in large numbers and when plants are covered by row covers or are growing in cold frames. The presence of aphids sometimes indicates that the plant is under stress—is the cabbage getting enough water, or sunlight, say? Check first to see if stress is a problem and then try to correct it. If there is a large infestation, look for aphid mummies and other natural enemies mentioned above. Mummies are swollen brown or metallic-looking aphids. Inside the mummy a wasp parasitoid is growing. They are valuable, so keep them. To remove aphids generally, wash the foliage with a strong blast of water and cut back the foliage if they persist. Fertilize and water the plant, and check on it in a few days. Repeat with the water spray a few more times. In extreme situations spray with insecticidal soap or a neem product.

A number of **beetles** are garden pests. They include asparagus beetles, Mexican bean beetles, different species of cucumber beetles, flea beetles, and wireworms (the larvae of click beetles). All are a problem throughout most of North America. Colorado potato beetles and Japanese beetles are primarily a problem in the eastern United States. Mexican bean beetles look like brown lady beetles with oval black spots; as their name implies, they feed on beans. Cucumber beetles are ladybug-like green or yellow-green beetles with either black stripes or black spots. Their larvae feed on the roots of corn and other vegetables. Adults devour members of the cucumber family, corn tassels, beans, and some salad greens. Flea beetles are minuscule black-and-white-striped beetles hardly big enough to be seen. The grubs feed on the roots and lower leaves of many vegetables, and the adults chew on the leaves of tomatoes, potatoes, radishes, peppers, and other plants—causing the leaves to look shot full of tiny holes. The adult click beetle is rarely seen, and its young, a brown, 1½-inch-long shiny larva called a wireworm, works underground and damages tubers, seeds, and roots. Colorado potato beetles are larger and rounder than lady beetles and have red-brown heads and black-and-yellow-striped backs. They are primarily a problem in the East, where they skeletonize the leaves of potatoes, tomatoes, and peppers. Japanese beetles, a problem east of the Mississippi, are fairly large metallic blue or green beetles with coppery wings. The larval stage (a grub) lives on the roots

of grasses, and the adult chews its way through beans and many ornamentals.

The larger beetles, if not present in great numbers, can be controlled by hand picking—in the morning is best, when the beetles are slower. Knock them into a bowl of soapy water. Flea beetles are too small to gather by hand; try a hand-held vacuum instead. Insecticidal soap on the underside of the leaves is also effective on flea beetles. Wireworms can be trapped by putting cut pieces of potatoes or carrots every five feet or so in the soil and then digging them up after a few days. Destroy the worms. Colorado potato beetles can be controlled, when young, by applications of *Bacillus thuringiensis* var. *san diego*, a beetle Bt that has also proven effective for flea beetles, as well.

Because most beetle species winter over in the soil, either as eggs or adults, crop rotation and fall cleanup becomes vital. New evidence indicates that beneficial nematodes are effective in controlling most beetles if applied during their soil-dwelling larval stage. Azadirachtin (the active ingredient in some formulations of neem) is also effective against the immature stage of most beetles and can act as a feeding deterrent for adults. Polyester row covers securely fastened to the ground can provide excellent control from most beetles. Obviously, row covers are of no use if the beetles are in a larval stage and ready to emerge from the soil under the row cover or if the adults are already established on the plant. This technique works best in combination with crop rotation. It has limited use on plants (such as cucumbers, squash, and melons) that need bees to pollinate the blooms, since bees also are excluded. Japanese beetle populations can also be reduced by applications of milky-spore, a naturally occurring soil-borne disease that infects the beetle in its grub stage—though the disease is slow to work. The grubs primarily feed in lawns; the application of lime, if your lawn is acidic, has been reported to help control grubs, too.

Caterpillars (sometimes called loopers and "worms") are the immature stage of moths and butterflies. Most pose no problem in our gardens and we encourage them to visit, but a few are a problem in the vegetable garden. The most notorious are the

tomato hornworm, beanloopers, cutworms, and the numerous cabbage worms and loopers that chew ragged holes in leaves. Natural controls include birds, wasps, and disease. Encourage birds by providing a birdbath, shelter, and berry-producing shrubs. Tolerate wasp nests if they're not a threat, and provide nectar plants for the miniwasps. Hand picking is very effective as well. The disease *Bacillus thuringiensis* var. *kurstaki* is available as a spray in a number of formulations. Brands include Bt *kurstaki*, Dipel, and Thuricide. It is a bacteria that, if applied when the caterpillar is fairly young, causes it to starve to death. Bt-k Bait contains the disease and lures budworms away from vegetables and to it. I seldom use Bt in any form, as it also kills all butterfly and harmless moth larvae. Cutworms are the caterpillar stage of various moth species. They are usually found in the soil and curl up into a ball when disturbed. Cutworms are a particular problem on annual vegetables when the seedlings first appear or when young transplants are set out. The cutworm often chews off the stem right at the soil line, killing the plant. Control cutworms by using cardboard collars or bottomless tin cans around the plant stem; be sure to sink these collars 1 inch into the ground. *Bacillus thuringiensis* gives limited control. Trichogramma miniwasps and black ground beetles are among cutworms' natural enemies and are often not present in a new garden.

Leaf miners tunnel through leaves, disfiguring them by causing patches of dead tissue where they feed; they do not burrow into the root. Leaf miners are the larvae of a small fly and can be controlled somewhat by neem or by applying beneficial nematodes.

Mites are among the few arachnids (spiders and their kin) that pose a problem. Mites are so small that a hand lens is usually needed to see them. They become a problem when they reproduce in great numbers. A symptom of serious mite damage is stippling on the leaves in the form of tiny white or yellow spots, sometimes accompanied by tiny webs. The major natural predators of pest mites are predatory mites, mite-eating thrips, and syrphid flies. Mites are most likely to thrive on dusty leaves and in warm weather. A routine foliage wash and misting of sensitive vegetables helps control mites. Mites are seldom a serious problem unless heavy-duty pesticides that kill off predatory mites have been used or plants are grown in the house. Cut back the plants and if you're using heavy-duty pesticides, stop the applications, and the balance could return. If all else fails, use the neem derivative, Green Light Fruit, Nut, and Vegetable Spray, or dispose of the plant.

Nematodes are microscopic round worms that inhabit the soil in most of the United States, particularly in the Southeast. Most nematode species live on decaying matter or are predatory on other nematodes, insects, or bacteria. A few types are parasitic, attaching themselves to the roots of plants. Edible plants particularly susceptible to nematode damage include beans, melons, lettuce, okra, pepper, squash, tomatoes, eggplant, and some perennial herbs. The symptoms of nematode damage are stunted-looking plants and small swellings or lesions on the roots.

Rotate annual vegetables with less-susceptible varieties; plant contaminated beds with a blanket of marigolds for a whole season; keep your soil high in organic matter (to encourage fungi and predatory nematodes, both of which act as biological controls); or if all else fails, grow edibles in containers with sterilized soil.

Snails and **slugs** are not insects, of course, but mollusks. They are especially fond of greens and seedlings of most vegetables. They feed at night and can go dormant for months in times of stress. In the absence of effective natural enemies (a few snail eggs are consumed by predatory beetles and earwigs), several snail-control strategies can be recommended. Since snails and slugs are most active after rain or irrigation, go out and destroy them on such nights. Only repeated forays provide adequate control. Hardwood ashes dusted around susceptible plants gives some control. Planter boxes with a strip of copper applied along the top perimeter boards effectively keep slugs and snails out; they won't cross the barrier. A word of warning: any overhanging leaves that can provide a bridge into the bed will defeat the barrier.

Whiteflies are sometimes a problem in mild-winter areas of the country, as well as in greenhouses nationwide, especially on lettuces, tomatoes, and cucumbers. Whiteflies can be a persistent problem if plants are against a building or fence, where air circulation is limited. In the garden, Encarsia wasps and other parasitoids usually provide adequate whitefly control. Occasionally, especially in cool weather or in greenhouses, whitefly populations may begin to cause serious plant damage (wilting and slowed growth or flowering). Look under the leaves to determine whether the scalelike, immobile larvae, the young crawling stage, or the pupae are present in large numbers. If so, wash them off with water from your hose. Repeat the washing three days in a row. In addition, try vacuuming up the adults with a handheld vacuum early in the day while the weather is still cool and they are less active. Insecticidal soap sprays can be quite effective as well.

Wildlife Problems

Rabbits and mice can cause problems for gardeners. To keep them out, use fine-weave fencing around the vegetable garden. If gophers or moles are a problem, plant large vegetables such as peppers, tomatoes, and squash in chicken wire baskets in the ground. Make the wire stick up a foot from the ground so the critters can't reach inside. In severe situations you might have to line whole beds with chicken wire. Gophers usually need to be trapped. Trapping for moles is less successful, but repellents like MoleMed sometimes help. Cats help with all rodent problems but seldom provide adequate control. Small, portable electric fences help keep raccoons, squirrels, and woodchucks out of the garden. Small-diameter wire mesh, bent into boxes and anchored with ground staples, protects seedlings from squirrels and chipmunks.

Deer are a serious problem—they love vegetables. I've tried myriad repellents, but they gave only short-term control. In some areas deer cause such severe problems that edible plants can't be grown without tall electric or nine-foot fences and/or an aggressive dog. The exception is herbs; deer don't feed on most culinary herbs.

Songbirds, starlings, and crows can be major pests of young seedlings, particularly lettuce, corn, and peas. Cover the emerging plants with bird netting and firmly anchor it to the ground so birds can't get under it and feast.

Pest Controls

Insecticidal soap sprays are effective against many pest insects, including caterpillars, aphids, mites, and whiteflies. They can be purchased, or you can make a soap spray at home. As a rule, I recommend purchasing insecticidal soaps, as they have been carefully formulated to give the most effective control and are less apt to burn your vegetables. If you do make your own, use a mild liquid dishwashing soap; not caustic detergents.

Neem-based pesticide and fungicide products, which are derived from the neem tree (*Azadirachta indica*), have relatively low toxicity to mammals but are effective against a wide range of insects. Neem products are considered "organic" pesticides by some organizations but not by others. Products containing a derivative of neem—azadirachtin—are effective because azadirachtin is an insect growth regulator that affects the ability of immature stages of insects such as leaf miners, cucumber beetles, and aphids to develop to adulthood. BioNeem and Azatin are commercial pesticides containing azadirachtin. Another neem product, Green Light Fruit, Nut, and Vegetable Spray, contains clarified hydrophobic extract of neem oil and is effective against mites, aphids, and some fungus diseases. Neem products are still fairly new in the United States. Although neem was at first thought to be harmless to beneficial insects, some studies now show that some parasitoid beneficial insects that feed on neem-treated pest insects were unable to survive to adulthood.

Pyrethrum, a botanical insecticide, is toxic to a wide range of insects but has relatively low toxicity to most mammals and breaks down quickly. The active ingredients in pyrethrum are pyrethins derived from chrysanthemum flowers. Do not confuse pyrethrum with pyrethoids, which are much more toxic synthetics that do not biodegrade as quickly. Many pyrethrums have a synergist, piperonyl butoxide (PBO), added to increase the effectiveness. As there is evidence that PBO may affect the human nervous system; try to use pyrethrums without PBO added. Wear gloves, goggles, and a respirator when using pyrethrum.

Diseases

Plant diseases are potentially far more damaging to your vegetables than are most insects. There are two types of diseases: those caused by nutrient deficiencies and those caused by pathogens. Diseases caused by pathogens, such as root rots, are difficult to control once they begin. Therefore, most plant disease control strategies feature prevention rather than control.

To keep diseases under control it is very important to plant the "right plant in the right place." For instance, salad greens in poorly drained soil often develop root rot. Tomatoes planted against a wall are prone to whiteflies and fungal diseases. Check the cultural needs of a plant before placing it in your garden. Proper light, air circulation, temperature, fertilization, and moisture are important factors in disease control. Finally, whenever possible, choose disease-resistant varieties when a particular pathogen is present or when conditions are optimal for the disease. The entries for individual plants in An Encyclopedia of Heirloom Vegetables (page 21) give specific cultural and variety information. As a final note, plants infected with disease pathogens should always be discarded, not composted.

Nutritional Deficiencies

For more basic information on plant nutrients, see the soil preparation information given in Appendix A (page 90). As with pathogens, the best way to solve nutritional problems is to prevent them. While there are mineral deficiencies that affect vegetables, most often caused by a pH that is below 6 or above 7.5, the most common nutritional deficiency is a lack of nitrogen. Vegetables need fairly high amounts of nitrogen in the soil to keep growing vigorously. Nitrogen deficiency is especially prevalent in soil that is sandy or low in organic matter. (Both clay and organic matter provide little nitrogen; they do hold on to it, however, thereby keeping it available to the plants' roots and keeping the nitrogen itself from leaching away.)

The main symptom of nitrogen deficiency is a pale and slightly yellow cast to the foliage, especially the lower, older leaves. For quick-growing crops like baby lettuces, by the time the symptoms show up, it's too late to apply a cure. You might as well pull out the plants and salvage what you can. To prevent the problem from recurring, supplement your beds with a good source of organic nitrogen like blood meal, chicken manure, or fish emulsion. For most vegetables, as they are going to be growing for a long season, correct the nitrogen deficiency by applying fish emulsion according to the directions on the container; reapply it in a month or so. (Usually nitrogen does not stay in the soil for more than four to six weeks, as it leaches out into the ground water.)

While I've stressed nitrogen deficiency, the real trick is to reach a good nitrogen balance in your soil; although plants must have nitrogen to grow, too much causes leaf edges to die, promotes succulent new growth savored by aphids, and makes plants prone to cold damage.

Diseases Caused by Pathogens

Anthracnose is a fungus that is primarily a problem in the eastern United States on beans, tomatoes, cucumbers, and melons. Affected plants develop spots on the leaves; furthermore, beans develop sunken black spots on the pods and stems, and melons, cucumbers, and tomatoes develop sunken spots on the fruits. The disease spreads readily in wet weather and overwinters in the soil on debris. Crop rotation, good air circulation, and choosing resistant varieties are the best defense. Neem-based Green Light Fruit, Nut and Vegetable Spray gives some control.

Blights and **bacterial diseases** include a number of diseases caused by fungi and bacteria that affect vegetables, and their names hint at the damage they do—such as blights, wilts, and leaf spots. As a rule, they are more of a problem in rainy and humid areas. Given the right conditions, they can be a problem in most of North America.

Early blight strikes tomatoes when plants are in full production or under stress and causes dark brown spots with rings in them on older leaves, which then turn yellow and die. Potato tubers are also prone to early blight and become covered with corky spots. Warm, moist conditions promote the disease. Late blight causes irregular gray spots on the tops of tomato leaves with white mold on the spots on the underside of the leaves. Leaves eventually turn brown and dry-looking. Fruits develop water-soaked spots that eventually turn corky. Potato tubers develop spots that eventually lead to rot. Cool nights with warm days in wet weather are ideal conditions for the disease. Halo and common blight cause spots on leaves and pods of most types of beans and are most active in wet weather. All these blight-causing fungi and bacteria overwinter on infected plant debris. To prevent infections, avoid overhead watering, clean up plant debris in the fall, rotate crops, and purchase only certified disease-free seed potatoes. Bacterial wilt affects cucumbers, melons, and sometimes squash. The disease is spread by cucumber beetles and causes the plants to wilt, then eventually die. To diagnose the disease, cut a wilted stem and look for milky sap that forms a thread when the tip of a stick touches it and is drawn away. The disease overwinters in cucumber beetles; cutting their population and installing floating row covers over young plants are the best defenses.

Damping off is caused by a parasitic fungus that lives near the soil surface and attacks young plants in their early seedling stage. It causes them to wilt and fall over just where they emerge from the soil. This fungus thrives under dark, humid conditions, so it can often be thwarted by keeping the seedlings in a bright, well-ventilated place in fast-draining soil. In addition, when possible, start seedlings in sterilized soil.

Fusarium wilt is a soil-borne fungus most prevalent in the warm parts of the country. It causes an overall wilting of the plant visible as the leaves from the base of the plant upward yellow and die. The plants most susceptible to different strains of the disease include tomatoes, potatoes, peppers, cucumber, squash, melons, and peas. While a serious problem in some areas, this disease can be controlled by planting only resistant varieties. Crop rotation is also helpful.

Mildews are fungal diseases that affect some vegetables—particularly peas, spinach, and squash—under certain conditions. There are two types of mildews: powdery and downy. Powdery mildew appears as a white powdery dust on the surface; downy mildew makes velvety or fuzzy white, yellow, or purple patches on leaves, buds, and tender stems. The poorer the air circulation and more humid the weather, the more apt your plants are to have downy mildew.

Make sure the plants have plenty of sun and are not crowded by other vegetation. If you must use overhead watering, do it in the morning. In some cases, powdery mildew can be washed off the plant. Do so early in the day, so that the plant has time to dry before evening. Powdery mildew is almost always present at the end of the season on squash and pea plants but is not a problem since they are usually through producing.

Lightweight "summer" horticultural oil combined with baking soda has proved effective against powdery mildew on some plants in research at Cornell University. Combine 1 tablespoon of baking soda and 2½ teaspoons of summer oil with 1 gallon of water. Spray weekly. Test on a small part of the plant first. Don't use horticultural oil on very hot days or on plants that are moisture-stressed; after applying the oil, wait at least a month before using any sulfur sprays on the same plant.

A "tea" for combating powdery mildew and possibly other disease-causing fungi can be made by wrapping a gallon of well-aged, manure-based compost in burlap and then steeping it in a 5-gallon bucket of water for about three days, in a warm place. Spray every three to four days, in the evening if possible, until symptoms disappear.

Downy mildew is sometimes a problem on lettuces, especially in late fall, in cold frames, and under row covers. Select resistant varieties when possible, try to keep irrigation water off the leaves, prevent plants from crowding, dispose of any infected leaves and plants, and, if growing greens in a cold frame make sure the air circulation is optimal.

Root rots and **crown rots** are caused by a number of different fungi. The classic symptom of root rot is wilting—even when a plant is well watered. Sometimes one side of the plant will wilt, more often the whole plant wilts. Affected plants are often stunted and yellow as well. The diagnosis is complete when the dead plant is pulled up to reveal rotten, black roots. Crown rot is a fungus that kills plants at the crown, and is primarily a problem in the Northeast. Root and crown rots are most often caused by poor drainage. There is no cure for root and crown rots once they involve the whole plant. Remove and destroy the plants and correct the drainage problem.

Verticillium wilt is a soil-borne fungus that can be a problem in most of North America, especially the cooler sections. The symptom of this disease is a sudden wilting of one part of or all of the plant. If you continually lose tomatoes or eggplants, this, or one of the other wilts, could be the problem. There is no cure, so plant resistant species or varieties if this disease is in your soil.

Viruses attack a number of plants. Symptoms are stunted growth and deformed or mottled leaves. The mosaic viruses destroy chlorophyll in the leaves, causing them to become yellow and blotched in a mosaic pattern. There is no cure for viral conditions, so the affected plants must be destroyed. Tomatoes, cucumbers, and beans are particularly susceptible. Viral diseases can be transmitted by aphids and leaf hoppers, or by seeds, so seed savers should be extra careful to learn the symptoms in individual plant species. When available, use resistant varieties.

resources

Gardening and Cooking Suppliers

Gardener's Supply Company
128 Intervale Road
Burlington, VT 05401
Gardening tools and supplies

The Natural Gardening
Company
217 San Anselmo Avenue
San Anselmo, CA 94960
Gardening supplies, organic fertilizers, beneficial nematodes

Native Seeds/SEARCH
526 North Fourth Avenue
Tucson, AZ 85705
Membership: $20.00
Low income/student: $12.00
Catalog: $1.00 for nonmembers
Selection of foodstuffs for cooking, including red and blue cornmeals, beans, and chile products; membership includes 10 percent discount on items in the catalog and the retail store in Tucson

Nutrite Inc.
P.O. Box 160
Elmira, Ontario
Canada N3B 2Z6
Good Canadian source of gardening supplies

Peaceful Valley Farm Supply
P.O. Box 2209
Grass Valley, CA 95945
Gardening supplies, organic fertilizers, seeds for cover crops

Old Sturbridge Village
Museum Gift Shop
1 Old Sturbridge Village Road
Sturbridge, MA 01566
Books and reproduction cooking equipment from the 1830s, including materials needed for open-hearth cooking, pottery bean pots, and traditional utensils

Sur La Table
Catalog Division
1765 Sixth Avenue South
Seattle, WA 98134
Cooking equipment

Williams-Sonoma
Mail Order Department
P.O. Box 7456
San Francisco, CA 94120
Cooking equipment

Wycliffe Gardens
P.O. Box 430
Kimberly, British Columbia
Canada V1A 2Y9
Good Canadian source of gardening supplies

Sources for Heirloom Seeds and Plants

Abundant Life Seed
Foundation
P. O. Box 772
Port Townsend, WA 98368
Nonprofit organization.
Membership: $30.00; Limited
income: $20.00
Catalog: $2.00 donation if not a
member
Specializes in open pollinated, heirloom, and endangered seeds

Becker's Seed Potatoes
R. R. 1
Trout Creek, ON
P0H 2L0 Canada
Certified seed potatoes; some heirlooms

Bountiful Gardens
18001 Shafer Ranch Road
Willits, CA 95490
Main Catalog: Free in U.S.;
$2.00 outside of U.S.
Rare seeds catalog: $2.00
Interesting selection of open-pollinated varieties, many from England; organic gardening supplies

Chiltern Seeds
Bortree Stile, Ulverston
Cumbria LA12 7PB
England
Salad greens, Oriental greens, herbs

The Cook's Garden
P. O. Box 535
Londonderry, VT 05148
Extensive selection of lettuces; superior varieties of vegetables and herbs

Corns
Rt. One, Box 32
Turpin, OK 73950
Carry open-pollinated dent, flint, and popcorns

DeGiorgi Company, Inc.
6011 North Street
Omaha, NB 68117
Catalog: $2.00
Vegetables, herbs, and flowers

The Digger's Club
Heronswood, 105 Latrobe
Parade
Dromana 3936
Australia
Seed exchange club and mail-order catalog with many old heirlooms

Filaree Farms
182 Conconully Highway
Okanogan, WA 98840
Specializes in many varieties of garlic

Flower and Herb Exchange
3076 North Winn Road
Decorah, IA 52101
Membership fee: $10.00
Rare and heirloom flower and herb seeds
Nonprofit organization dedicated to saving diversity; members join an extensive network of gardeners saving and exchanging seeds

Fox Hollow Seeds
P. O. Box 148
McGrann, PA 16236
Catalog: $1.00
Specializes in heirloom herbs, vegetables, flowers

Fred's Plant Farm
4589 Ralston Road
Martin, TN 38237
Carries a nice selection of old sweet potato varieties

Garden City Seeds
778 Highway 93 North
Hamilton, MT 59840
Specializes in varieties for short seasons and cold climates

The Gourmet Gardener
8650 College Boulevard
Overland Park, KS 66210
*Some heirlooms, many European
varieties; herbs, vegetables, and
edible flower seeds*

Gleckler's Seedsman
Metamora, OH 43540
*Open-pollinated heirlooms plus a
large selection of Native
American squash*

Harris Seeds and Nursery
P. O. Box 22960
Rochester, NY 14692
*Carries heirloom vegetable, herb,
and flower seeds from the Genesee
Country Village and Museum*

Heirloom Seeds
P. O. Box 245
West Elisabeth, PA 15088-0245
Catalog: $1.00
*Specializes in heirloom and open-
pollinated varieties; all seeds
untreated*

Henry Field's Seed and Nursery
Company
415 North Burnett
Shenandoah, IA 51602
*Large variety of vegetables, some
heirlooms*

Heritage Seed Company
HC Box 187
Star City, AZ 71667
*Organically grown alliums,
specialty onion list*

High Altitude Gardens
P. O. Box 4619
Ketchum, ID 83340
*Open pollinated seeds for short,
cold seasons and high altitudes*

J. L. Hudson, Seedsman
Star Route 2, Box 337
La Honda, CA 94020
For catalog: P. O. Box 1058,
Redwood City, CA 94064
Catalog: $1.00
*Open-pollinated; heirlooms;
unusual varieties*

Johnny's Selected Seeds
Foss Hill Road
Albion, ME 04910
*Excellent selection of herb and
vegetable seeds; unusual varieties*

Landis Valley Museum
Heirloom Seed Project
2451 Kissel Hill Road,
Lancaster, PA 17601
Catalog: $4.00 U.S.; $5.00 out-
side U.S.
*Heirloom seeds of herbs, vegeta-
bles, flowers, and cover crops*

D. Landreth Seed Company
180 W. Ostend St.
P. O. Box 6426
Baltimore, MD 21230
*Vegetables, herbs, flowers; includ-
ing ethnic and heirloom varieties*

Liberty Seed Company
P. O. Box 806
New Philadelphia, OH 44663
*Lots of vegetable varieties includ-
ing some heirlooms*

Lockhart Seeds, Inc.
P. O. Box 1361
3 North Wilson Way
Stockton, CA 95205
Price list only, no catalog.
*Some vegetable seeds; many onion
varieties; seed potatoes*

Native Seeds/SEARCH
526 North Fourth Avenue
Tucson, AZ 85705
Membership: 20.00
Low income/student: $12.00
Catalog: $1.00 for nonmembers
*Nonprofit organization dedicated
to preservation of traditional
crops, seeds, and farming methods
of the native peoples of the U.S.
Southwest and northern Mexico.
Membership includes: Quarterly
newsletter; seed catalog; 10 percent discount on items in the catalog and the retail store in Tucson*

Nichols Garden Nursery
1190 North Pacific Highway NE
Albany, OR 97321-4580
Wide selection of interesting vari-

eties, including heirlooms and
European varieties

Old Sturbridge Village
Museum Gift Shop
1 Old Sturbridge Village Road
Sturbridge, MA 01566
*Seeds of early nineteenth century
flowers and vegetables, most are
especially good for Northern gardens; books, some cooking equipment - reproductions from the 1830s*

The Pepper Gal
P. O. Box 23006
Ft. Lauderdale, FL 33307-3006
Catalog: $2.00
*Great selection of hot, sweet, and
ornamental peppers*

Pinetree Garden Seeds
Box 300
New Gloucester, ME 04260
*Good selection of heirloom and
other open-pollinated varieties*

Plants of the Southwest
Agua Fria, Route 6, Box 11A
Santa Fe, NM 87501
Catalog: $3.50
*Open-pollinated seeds of warm
season vegetables, heirlooms,
grasses, and wild flowers*

Plimouth Plantation
Mail Order Department
P. O. Box 1620
Plymouth, MA 02362
*Seeds of herbs and vegetables used
in the kitchen gardens of seven-
teenth century Plymouth, also
native plants of the area.*

Redwood City Seed Company
P. O. Box 361
Redwood City, CA 94064
Catalog: $1.00 in U.S., Canada,
Mexico; $2.00 to other countries
*Specializes in endangered culti-
vated plants*

Renee's Garden
Look for seed racks in better
retail nurseries. For more information, call toll-free (888) 880-
7228 or look for her on-line at
garden.com/reneesgarden.

Ronniger's Seed & Potato Co.
P. O. Box 307
Ellensburg, WA 98926
*Certified organic seed potatoes
and certified disease-free seed
potatoes*

Sand Hill Preservation Center
Heirloom Seeds and Poultry
1878 230th Street
Calamus, IA 52729
*Major source for heirloom sweet
potatoes and squashes*

Santa Barbara Heirloom
Nursery
P. O. Box 4235
Santa Barbara, CA 93140
*Certified organically grown
heirloom seedlings*

Seeds Blum
HC 33 Box 2057
Boise, ID 83706
Catalog: $3.00; first-class
option: $5.00
*Large selection of heirloom veg-
etables and unusual salad greens*

Seeds of Change
P. O. Box 15700
Santa Fe, NM 87506
*Organically grown vegetable and
herb seeds*

Seed Savers Exchange
3076 North Winn Road
Decorah, IA 52101
Membership fee: $25.00
Low income/Senior/Student:
$20.00; Canadian: $30.00
Overseas: $40.00
*Rare and heirloom vegetable
seeds. Catalog for purchasing
selected seeds is free to nonmem-
bers and members. Nonprofit
organization dedicated to saving
diversity. Members join an extensive network of gardeners saving
and exchanging seeds.*

Select Seeds Antique Flowers
180 Stickney Road
Union, CT 06076
Catalog: $1.00

*Specializes in species and antique
flower seeds*

Shepherd's Garden Seeds
30 Irene Street
Torrington, CT 06790
*Superior varieties of European
and heirloom varieties*

R. H. Shumway's
P. O. Box 1
Graniteville, SC 29829
*Carries many open-pollinated
vegetable and flower varieties,
many adapted to Southern gardens*

Southern Exposure Seed
Exchange
P. O. Box 170
Earlysville, VA 22936
Catalog: $2.00
*Specializes in heat tolerant vari-
eties; carries a wide selection of
well researched heirlooms*

Steele Plant Farm
Box 191, Gleason, TN 38229
*Specializes in sweet potatoes,
onions, brassicas; ship in the spring*

Territorial Seed Company
P. O. Box 157
Cottage Grove, OR 97424-0061
*Good selection of heirloom and
other open-pollinated varieties*

The Thomas Jefferson Center
for Historic Plants
Monticello
P. O. Box 316
Charlottesville, VA 22902
Catalog: $1.00
*Heirloom, vegetable, herb, and
flower seeds, including offspring
of original Monticello plantings*

Thompson & Morgan, Ltd.
Poplar Lane, Ipswich
Suffolk 1P8 3BU
England
Wide variety of types of seeds

Tomato Growers Supply
Company
P. O. Box 2237
Fort Meyers, FL 33902

*Extensive selection of all types of
tomatoes*

Totally Tomatoes
P. O. Box 1626
Augusta, GA 30903
Extensive selection of tomatoes

Synergy Seeds
P. O. Box 323
Orleans, CA 95556
*Homegrown heirlooms specializ-
ing in those adapted to
Mediterranean climate of
California*

Vermont Bean Seed Company
Garden Lane
Fair Haven, VT 05743
*Selection of vegetables seeds
including many types of beans*

Willhite Seed Company Inc.
P. O. Box 23
Poolville, TX 76487
*Big selection of Southern peas and
melons; good selection of squashes
and other warm weather crops*

Wood Prairie Farm
49 Kinney Road
Bridgewater, ME 04735
*Certified organic seed potatoes;
also organic vegetables and grains
for cooking*

Historic Demonstration Gardens

Genesee Country Village and
Museum
P.O. Box 310
Mumford, NY 14511
*A restored village depicting life in
western New York's Genesee
Valley in the 1800s; to order seeds
of the heirloom varieties grown in
the gardens, see Harris Seeds and
Nursery in "Sources of Heirloom
Seeds and Plants"*

Heritage Farm
Seed Savers Exchange
3076 North Winn Road
Decorah, IA 52101
Historical orchard and preserva-

*tion gardens where nearly two
thousand heirloom vegetable
varieties and seven hundred different apple varieties are grown; gift
shop carries seeds and books*

Landis Valley Museum
2451 Kissel Hill Road
Lancaster, PA 17601
*Historical buildings, farmsteads
with animals, and working gardens displaying Pennsylvania
German rural heritage*

Monticello
Department of Public Affairs
P.O. Box 316
Charlottesville, VA 22902
*The restored home, orchards, and
gardens of Thomas Jefferson are
open to visitors year-round; the
gift store carries books, seeds, and
items from his time*

The National Colonial Farm
The Accokeek Foundation
3400 Bryan Point Road
Accokeek, MD 20607
*A demonstration farm across the
Potomac River from Mount
Vernon that includes re-created
buildings and gardens; cooking
and planting demonstrations;
crops grown here were used by
settlers in Maryland during the
late colonial period (ca. 1775)*

Native Seeds/SEARCH
Demonstration Garden
Tucson Botanical Gardens
2150 North Alvernon Way
Tucson, AZ 85712
*Historical gardens demonstrating
plants and gardening techniques
used by the Southwest Native
Americans; gift shop carries books,
some cooking equipment, baskets,
and seeds*

Old Sturbridge Village
Museum Gift Shop
1 Old Sturbridge Village Road
Sturbridge, MA 01566
*Reconstructed 1830s town with
historical vegetable, herb, and
flower gardens; garden and cook-*

*ing demonstrations vary with the
day and season; country fair fea-
turing heirloom vegetables every
fall; extensive gift shop with
books, seeds, and authentic cooking implements*

Plimoth Plantation
P.O. Box 1620
Plymouth, MA 02362
*Living history museum includes a
village depicting life at Plymouth
in 1627; food demonstrations,
including special visitor dining
events, and display settler and
Wampanoag Native American
gardens with interpretations; gift
shops offer books and seeds*

Pounder Heritage Vegetable
Garden
Cornell University
Cornell Plantations
One Plantations Road
Ithaca, NY 14850
*Demonstration gardens from
Colonial times to the present; dis-
play gardens show the evolution in
the domestication of a different
vegetable each year*

Bibliography

Abell, Mrs. L. G. *The Skilful
Housewife's Book, or
Complete Guide to Domestic
Cookery, Taste, Comfort, and
Economy.* New York: D.
Newell, 1846.

Adams, Marcia. *Marcia Adams'
Heirloom Recipes: Yesterday's
Favorites, Tomorrow's
Treasures.* New York:
Clarkson Potter Publishers,
1994.

Andrus, Silas. *The Experienced
American Housekeeper.* 1829.

Ashworth, Suzanne. *Seed to
Seed: Seed Saving Techniques
for the Vegetable Gardener.*
Decorah, Iowa.: Seed Saver
Publications, 1991.

Bubel, Nancy. *The New Seed Starters Handbook*. Emmaus, Pa.: Rodale Press, 1988.

Burr, Fearing Jr. *Field and Garden Vegetables of America*. 1865. Reprint, Chillicothe, Ill.: American Botanist, 1994.

Carr, Anna. *Rodale's Color Handbook of Garden Insects*. Emmaus, Pa.: Rodale Press, 1979.

Carter, Susannah. *The Frugal Housewife*. New York: Rogers and Berry, 1792.

Cathey, H. Marc, and Linda Bellamy. *Heat-Zone Gardening: How to Choose Plants That Thrive in Your Region's Warmest Weather*. Alexandria, Va.: Time-Life Books, 1998.

Child, Lydia Maria. *The American Frugal Housewife Dedicated to Those Who Are Not Ashamed of Economy*. 12th ed. Boston: Carter, Hendee, and Co., 1832.

Clarke, Ethne. *The Art of the Kitchen Garden*. New York: Knopf, 1987.

Cornucopia: A Source Book for Edible Plants. Vista, Calif.: Kampong Publications, 1990.

Costenbader, Carol W. *The Big Book of Preserving the Harvest*. Pownal, Vt.: Story Communications, 1997.

Editors of Sunset Books and Sunset Magazine. *Sunset National Garden Book*. Menlo Park, Calif.: Sunset Books, 1997.

Fisher, Abby. *What Mrs. Fisher Knows About Old Southern Cooking*. 1881. Reprint, with historical notes by Karen Hess, Bedford, Mass.: Applewood Books, 1995.

Fowler, Cary and Pat Mooney. *Shattering: Food, Politics, and the Loss of Genetic Diversity*. Tucson: University of Arizona Press, 1990.

Fussell, Betty. *The Story of Corn: The Myths and History, The Culture and Agriculture, The Art and Science of America's Quintessential Crop*. New York: Knopf, 1992.

Gardner, Jo Ann. *The Heirloom Garden: Selecting and Growing over 300 Old-Fashioned Ornamentals*. Pownal, Vt.: Storey Communications, 1992.

Gilkeson, Linda, Pam Peirce, and Miranda Smith. *Rodale's Pest and Disease Problem Solver: A Chemical-Free Guide to Keeping Your Garden Healthy*. Emmaus, Pa.: Rodale Press, 1996.

Glasse, Hannah. *The Art of Cookery Made Plain and Easy*. 1805. Reprint, with historical notes by Karen Hess, Bedford, Mass.: Applewood Books, 1997.

Kavasch, E. Barrie. *Native Harvests: Recipes and Botanicals of the Amerian Indian*. New York: Vintage Books, 1979.

Kitchener, William. *The Cook's Oracle*. Boston: Munroe and Francis, 1823.

Lee, Mrs. N. K. M. *The Cook's Own Book*. Boston: Munroe and Francis, 1832.

McMahon, Bernard. *The American Gardener's Calendar*. 1806. Reprint, Charlottesville, Va.: Thomas Jefferson Memorial Foundation, 1997.

Nabhan, Gary Paul. *Enduring Seeds: Native American Agriculture and Wild Plant Conservation*. San Francisco: North Point Press, 1989.

National Gardening Association. *Gardening: The Complete Guide to Growing America's Favorite Fruits and Vegetables*. Reading, Mass.: Addison-Wesley, 1986.

Ogden, Shepherd. *Step by Step Organic Vegetable Gardening: The Gardening Classic Revised and Updated*. New York: HarperCollins, 1992.

Olkowski, William, Sheila Daar, and Helga Olkowski. *The Gardener's Guide to Common-Sense Pest Control*. Newtown, Conn.: Taunton Press, 1995.

Reilly, Ann. *Park's Success with Seeds*. Greenwood, S.C.: Geo. W. Park Seed Co., 1978.

Rogers, Marc. *Saving Seeds: The Gardener's Guide to Growing and Storing Vegetable and Flower Seeds*. Pownal, Vt.: Storey Communications, 1990.

Simmons, Amelia. *American Cookery*. 1796. Reprint of 2d edition, Bedford, Mass.: Applewood Books, 1996.

Sloat, Caroline, ed. *Old Sturbridge Village Cookbook*. Old Saybrook, Conn.: Globe Pequot Press, 1984.

Smith, Jeff. *The Frugal Gourmet on Our Immigrant Ancestors: Recipes You Should Have Gotten from Your Grandmother*. New York: Morrow and Company, 1990.

Stickland, Sue. *Heirloom Vegetables: A Home Gardener's Guide to Finding and Growing Vegetables from the Past*. New York: Fireside Books, 1998.

acknowledgments

My garden is the foundation for my books, photography, and recipes. For nearly twelve months of the year, we toil to keep it beautiful and bountiful. Unlike most gardens, as it is a photo studio and trial plot, it must look glorious, be healthy, and produce for the kitchen all year. To complicate the maintenance, all the beds are changed at least twice a year. Needless to say, it is a large undertaking. For two decades, a quartet of talented organic gardener/cooks have not only given it hundreds of hours of loving attention, but they have also been generous with their vast knowledge of plants. Together we have forged our concept of gardening and cooking, much of which I share with you in this series of garden cookbooks.

I wish to thank Wendy Krupnick for giving the garden such a strong foundation and Joe Queirolo for maintaining it for many years and lending it such a gentle and sure hand. For the past decade, Jody Main and Duncan Minalga have helped me expand my garden horizons. No matter how complex the project, they enthusiastically rise to the occasion. In the kitchen, I am most fortunate to have Gudi Riter, a very talented cook who developed many of her skills in Germany and France. I thank her for the help she provides as we create recipes and present them in all their glory.

I thank Dayna Lane for her steady hand and editorial assistance. In addition to day-to-day compilations, she joins me on our constant search for the most effective organic pest controls, superior herb varieties, and the best sources for plants.

Gardeners are by nature most generous. I want to thank Carole Saville, who keeps me up to date, no matter how esoteric the plant or recipe; David Cavagnaro, Kent and Diane Whealy, Jan Blum, and Mahina Drees, who are willing to share their vast knowledge of heirloom vegetables; Renee Shepherd, of Renee's Garden Seeds, and Shep Ogden, of the Cook's Garden, who are always available to answer vegetable variety information; the folks at Apple Wood books for providing many of the old cookbooks; and the great folks at Old Sturbridge Village—Christie White, Debra Freidman, and Deidre Goguen, who made themselves available for numerous interviews and photo sessions and who answered countless questions.

I would also like to thank my husband, Robert, who gives such quality technical advice and loving support, and Nancy Favier for her occasional help in the garden and office.

Many people were instrumental in bringing this book project to fruition. They include Jane Whitfield, Linda Gunnarson, and David Humphrey, who were integral to the initial vision of this book; Kathryn Sky-Peck, for providing the style and quality of the layout; and Marcie Hawthorne, for the lovely drawings. Heartfelt thanks to Eric Oey and to the entire Periplus staff, especially Deane Norton, Jan Johnson, and Sonia MacNeil, for their help. Finally, I would like to thank my editor, Isabelle Bleecker, for her gentle guidance, attention to detail, and thoughtful presence.